341 to Bryher and Trosco   Sept- Oct 2004

341 to Bryher and Trosco   Sept- Oct 2004

TRESCO TIMES

THE LAST PIECE OF ENGLAND

RICHARD BARBER

HALSGROVE

First published in Great Britain in 2002

British Library Cataloguing-in-Publication Data
A CIP record for this title is available from the British Library

ISBN 1 84114 163 1

HALSGROVE
Halsgrove House
Lower Moor Way
Tiverton, Devon EX16 6SS
Tel: 01884 243242
Fax: 01884 243325
email: sales@halsgrove.com
website: www.halsgrove.com

Printed and bound by
Bookcraft Ltd, Midsomer Norton

CONTENTS

ACKNOWLEDGEMENTS

Many people have helped and encouraged this attempt at capturing the *genus loci* of Tresco. First I must tug the forelock in the direction of Robert and Lucy Dorrien Smith who generously offered me access to their photographic archive at the Abbey. The largest number of photographs has come from that source. Many had been taken by various members of the Gibson family, and I am grateful to Sandra Gibson-Kyne for allowing me permission to reproduce them in this book, and also for providing many more where there were gaps.

Several islanders opened up their own photo albums and let me publish photographs – Mike and Isobel Nelhams, Gloria Lawry, Nonie Handy, Eddie Birch, Kate Parkes, who so sadly died before she could see them in print, Roger and Ann Oyler, Roy and Eve Cooper. I must make a special mention of Roy the former postmaster who acts as the island's archivist and historian. I very nearly went insane trying to sort out family history – the Smiths, the Dorriens, the Dorrien Smiths, the Smith Dorriens, the Smith Dorrien Smiths… Roy patiently sorted it for me. I think I got it right, but any mistakes are mine not his. He also lent me many photos from the period of the Great War, and the long letter from A. E. Bull who was stationed here.

Wars have always cast their shadow on Tresco, and the Second World War saw Special Forces missions being carried out from New Grimsby. It was a huge honour to meet Sir Brooks Richards, formerly of SOE, and others of his shipmates who came to Tresco to unveil a plaque in honour of their exploits. Sir Brooks has written a book about SOE and SIS's work on Tresco and along the coasts of Europe during the war. He kindly let me use photographs and text from his book *Secret Flotillas* – which is an excellent read and is about to be republished. At the unveiling ceremony in New Grimsby in July 2000 was Julia Garnett, widow of John Garnett. She offered me John's unpublished reminiscences and photos for which I am most grateful.

Kathy Todd's evocative painting of the author and his sailing companion that adorns the cover of the book is reproduced with the permission of the artist. Matt Lethbridge, former coxswain of the St Mary's lifeboat, similarly gave permission for me to use his paintings of the *Isabo* and *Mando*. Vaughan Ives took the photograph of the author on the back cover. Other photographs or illustrations came from the Fleet Air Arm Museum and the United Kingdom Hydrographic Office.

The charts appearing on pages 16 and 17 are © [British] Crown Copyright 2001. Published by permission of the Controller of Her Majesty's Sationery Office and the UK Hydrographic Office (www.ukho.gov.uk).

I must also thank Danny Baker for his permission to reprint his very funny piece from the Sports Section of *The Times*, and Rad Petrovic for allowing me to reprint her Tresco *Guardian* piece.

I hope that I have remembered to thank everyone. My deepest apologies to anyone I have inadvertently missed.

Setting off on a family picnic, New Grimsby, 1905.

INTRODUCTION

Land's End is the most westerly tip of mainland England – at the very end of the Cornish peninsula. Thirty miles beyond Land's End in the Western Approaches to the English Channel are the Isles of Scilly. The last piece of England before America.

Scilly is an extraordinary group of islands and rocks that must have been the peaks of hills before the inundation of the sea that now covers the lost land of Lyonesse that was reputed to lie between Scilly and Land's End. Scilly is a magical place that tugs at the heart of everyone who visits the islands. The mists of myth and legend that shroud the islands only add to their attraction.

Many believe that King Arthur and a number of his knights found eternal rest here – Lancelot, Tristram, Banyan, Bor, Ector, Caradoc and Percival. They were all that remained of the chivalry of Britain after Mordred had slain Arthur.

This noble band was pursued by the vengeful Mordred and his army across Cornwall and onto the plains of Lyonesse. They fled west towards the hills of Cassiteris. It was then that the Great Enchanter, Merlin, confronted Mordred. Raising his arm, the wizard Merlin caused the earth to tremble, and then sink below the level of the ocean. With a ghastly roar the sea rushed onto the plain and Mordred and his army were swept away in a boiling maelstrom of waves.

On the hills of Cassiteris, later to be known as Scilly, the Knights of the Round Table dismounted, knelt on the turf and thanked God for their deliverance. They were safe on what was now an island – separated from the mainland by 30 miles of turbulent sea. The land of Lyonesse that once lay between them and Cornwall had vanished, together with all its churches, villages and pastures.

That is one of the old legends of Lyonesse.

Later, the monks of the great Abbey at Glastonbury in Somerset claimed to have found King Arthur's tomb in their grounds, but others prefer to believe that his body was brought to Scilly – the magical islands of the west – to be buried. Certainly, there are two uninhabited islands in Scilly that have carried his name for centuries.

In the 1,500 years from Arthur's time to the present much has happened on Scilly, but little has changed the timeless beauty of these gentle islands. Two millennia before Arthur was born, Bronze Age people considered Scilly a sacred spot, and many of their religious structures are still there for us to see – a ritual landscape that was ancient even in Arthur's time.

In 1991 I came to live and work on Tresco, one of the five inhabited islands of Scilly.

What follows is a compilation of some of the pieces that we published in the *Tresco Times*, to which has been added many unpublished archive photographs and stories from Scilly's past that have been passed on by islanders, or recorded in faded newspaper cuttings from long ago.

Much has had to be left out, far more than I was able to include. We only scoop the surface of a deep pool. This is not a definitive community history, but a personal, sometimes wry look at a way of life that has long vanished on the mainland.

It's all about the Last Piece of England.

To my friends on Scilly

CHAPTER ONE

ARRIVING ON TRESCO

The private island of Tresco is roughly two miles long by half-a-mile wide, has only about 130 permanent residents, and since the 1830s has been leased from the Duchy of Cornwall by the Smith Dorrien Smith family.

I first visited Tresco in 1978, and then returned with my American painter wife, Kathy, 13 years later to take up a job as manager of Tresco's holiday cottages.

Tresco from the air.

It was an October day in 1991 when we reached Penzance. We dropped off the hire car in the town and took a taxi to the heliport – a low single-storey building with a hangar and a grass field separated from the main road by a wooden fence. It had a friendly rural feel; the staff smiled and had healthy tans; the passengers seeming grey by comparison, after the long drive to the tip of Cornwall.

The helicopter seated nearly 30 people and every seat was taken as we lifted off from the grass field in a gentle stepped ascent. Below, the roof of a supermarket glinted in the sun, and soon we looked out at the mass of St Michael's Mount on one side and Penzance on the other as we headed west over the Cornish peninsula to Land's End. At last we relaxed; on our way to a new life on a small island. No longer did we need to own a car, a house – or a mortgage. Life would be simple and uncomplicated.

We flew over the patchwork fields of Penwith, the most westerly district in mainland England. Below us, the fields were marked by stone 'hedges' most of which had been laid by Bronze Age men to mark their boundaries.

'We flew over the patchwork fields of Penwith'.

The Longships lighthouse passed beneath us, marking the final tip of the mainland, and we started out across 40 miles of angry sea. 500 metres below the sea was streaked by wind, and clumps of brown seaweed, ripped from rocks, floated just below the surface.

Fifteen minutes later we landed on Tresco. The helicopter alighted on a well-cut field that appeared to double as a cricket ground. We had landed next to the Abbey Garden where luxuriant sub-tropical foliage hinted at all kinds of exotic plants. Behind the Garden sat the Abbey – a granite Victorian pile built in the fashion of many similar properties in Scotland. A Union flag flew high from a flag-staff. At the end of the building was a stone tower. This contained the Tower Flat where we were to be quartered until a suitable cottage became available.

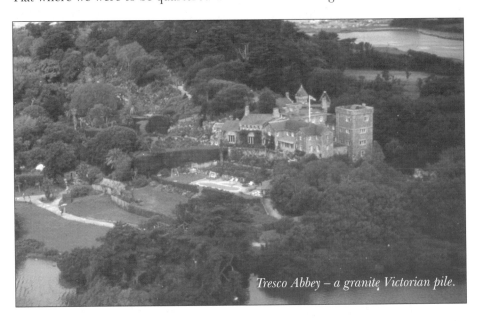

Tresco Abbey – a granite Victorian pile.

Along with the other passengers – holidaymakers mostly – we collected our bags from outside the garden-shed structure that was both 'control tower' and 'terminal'. We took our seats on a covered trailer towed by a tractor. The helicopter and its raucous clatter disappeared back to Penzance, and the total silence of the island descended like a curtain.

It's hard to describe the effect of total silence. Very few people experience it – the sound of neighbours, traffic, aircraft is almost totally pervasive in the 21st century. On Tresco one arrives with the din of the helicopter ringing in one's ears, and then a few minutes later – perfect peace and tranquillity.

We sat waiting for the tractor driver. We were now on island time. People were unhurried. Our driver was one of the fire-crew so could not be dismissed to drive us until the helicopter was several miles away. We listened to the calls of the birds in the trees as we sat on the trailer in the afternoon sunshine. Then after a few minutes we were on our way.

Tractor-drawn trailer at the heliport.

Five minutes later we stood with our bags in the Tower Flat – up a flight of stairs from the courtyard of the Abbey. Outside, the sun illuminated the brown gorse with golden warmth. Beyond lay the vivid blue of the sea and the distant Eastern Isles. We looked down from the Tower on a view that contained a clarity and variation of colour that neither of us had experienced.

"A drink!" I said.

The ice cubes crackled as the pale brown Malt covered them. We each took a glass and sank into a well-stuffed chair.

Outside the evening sun faded and a rosy glow touched the cream clouds. The blue of the sky was now a pale Cambridge shade. It seemed too good to be true – as if a Hollywood film director had lit the landscape with an improbable beauty.

The sun had gone when we turned off the light that night. The first stars were visible, bright against the velvet sky. In the silent night we slept the sleep enjoyed by the young, the old, and those who have travelled all day – and it had been a long day.

Next morning after breakfast, we left the flat to spend our first day on the island. We were about to meet our first islander.

In the large back hall of the Abbey, a couple of big deep-freezes murmured quietly. Various crates were stacked neatly around.

Almost hidden behind the open door of a large cupboard a pair of legs encased in gumboots was visible. I waited. Eventually, the cupboard door swung back and a stocky man in glasses stood up. He observed us without comment.

"Good morning." I said.

"Morning." This without even a glance at us.

He busied himself with a long stick cut from a sapling. It was probably about 8 foot long, and he was busy splitting the top of it with a large penknife. Finally, he finished. Only then did he look at us.

"This should do it," he said.

He took a slice of white bread out his pocket and fixed it in the splice he had made at the top of the stick. He looked at it proudly, and waved it about. It swished like a good fishing-rod, and the bread stayed firmly fixed in the splice.

"Perfect."

Looking back now, I cannot remember what I thought he might be about to do with his creation. I think I imagined it to be some kind of arcane Scillonian fishing implement.

Perhaps the islanders – when their long day was over – eked out their meals

An inviting lane between two cottages.

Some interesting-looking stones in profile against the skyline.

A gateway, with a post that looked like it might have been stolen from a stone circle, framed the nearby rock-island of Men a Vaur.

Either the weather or the hand of man had created the mark of a cross.

with eels caught with long poles and bits of bread. The truth was rather different and more bizarre.

"Come on," he said, and shot out of the door with the pole. We followed.

In the large gravel courtyard that formed the forecourt of the Abbey, he suddenly turned and introduced himself. "I'm the Abbey odd-job man."

Without waiting for a response he swooped round the yard, waving the stick high above him, the bread flashing white in the sunshine. All the while he made a strange high-pitched whistle. Some island men passed the gatehouse, looked at him, grimaced and laughed.

"What exactly are you doing?" Kathy asked him, in a strange voice that suggested she might know the answer.

"Trying to feed the birds," he said happily.

"Let's get out of here," muttered Kathy nervously.

We walked on down the drive. Above us the trees bent to a mild breeze. Although it was late October, it felt warm and autumnal. There was no hint of winter in the air. At the end of the drive, the channel of water separating the neighbouring island of Bryher was a dark blue, reflecting the sky above. There wasn't a cloud in the sky.

We walked up a concrete road past Tresco Stores to the top of the hill and took an inviting puddled lane between two cottages that lead towards fields.

Some interesting-looking stones stood out in profile against the skyline.

The lane took us to a T-junction. To the left was a line of islanders' white-washed cottages. To the right, the lane was banked high and lush with wild garlic. It curved out of sight, tempting us to follow...

We walked round the curve of the lane and stopped at a field-gate. A gate-post that looked like it might have been stolen from a stone circle framed the nearby rock-island of Men a Vaur. The deep green of the field rose up to the bright blue skyline. Leaning on the gate, with the light scent of wild garlic on the air and the sun warm on our backs, we had stepped back several hundred years. This unmade lane had been there since pre-history, off to our left a row of cottages were at least three hundred years old, and the stones on the hill above us must have been placed there a couple of millennia past.

The lonely cry of a curlew added to the feeling of remoteness. Nothing from the twentieth century intruded.

"According to the map," I said, opening it up "these stones have the good circular name of Dial Rocks. Stone circle, maybe?"

We climbed over the gate and walked up the hill. The grass was lush and thick. A herd of inquisitive bullocks looked up from their cropping to stare at us. Near the top of the hill we came up to the largest of the stones. All around it the cattle had worn out a circle of dirt in the grass, drawn to it as we were. It had that kind of magnetic property.

The stone was a peculiar shape, and as we got close we saw that it was three stones – one on top of the other. On it, either the weather or the hand of man had created the mark of a cross.

We had thought this stone to be positioned on top of the hill, but in fact it stood well below the summit. We stroked its rough granite surface, and looked out at the spectacular view that extended over most of the Isles of Scilly. To the east lay the island of St Martin's and beyond that the mysterious Eastern Isles that we had looked down on from the Tower. To the south lay St Mary's and St Agnes, and to the west we could see Samson and Bryher. In the field other stones stood erect.

A vast pyramid hill with a stone spine rose from the ground.

"Stay a minute," I said. "Let's just take it in."

Down below, exactly due east, the church's Christian orientation pointed up to where we stood. The two stone crosses on the gable ends stood in line like rifle sights.

North of the church, behind the hotel, a vast pyramid hill with a stone spine rose from the ground.

The landscape felt connected, and we felt part of it.

Three vast stones piled precisely on each other.

Walking to the top of the field we came to a stone wall and clambered over to find ourselves in a totally different environment.

We had stepped further back in time and crossed into the Bronze Age North End.

The pastureland on the hill and the little valley now lay behind us. We had walked through the gateway of Dial Rocks and entered a magical ritual landscape above.

We came across three vast stones, each weighing several tons, piled precisely on each other.

A line of equally large stones were placed in a line leading away from this marker.

Following the line and then cresting a small rise we came to the edge of the cliff. There, pointing back exactly the way we had come, sat another huge stone. It looked like a huge squatting bird.

Beyond, the North End stretched away – a glorious multicoloured carpet of green, blue, purple and yellow. It stretched about half a mile in each direction before cliffs dropped down to the sea. To the west were the ruins of King Charles's Castle, but otherwise nothing had been built here for three or four thousand years – yet the hand of Bronze Age Man was visible everywhere.

Large stones were placed in a line leading away from this marker.

At first glance the carpet of colour was broken only by random rocks and boulders. Soon, it was possible to pick out the mounds of graves and alignments of stones. We started our march across the moorland.

The carpet of heather sank under each step, and we kept our eyes down looking for the next footstep. After a while it was like looking down on a miniature forest, each heather plant like a tree and we felt like giants. The rocks strewn over the plateau were not large, few more than a couple of feet high. Two shapes of stones appeared repeatedly across this landscape. One was shaved down one side as if to provide a sight-line, the other was shaped like a triangular pyramid. Other stones had water-gathering basins carved out of them that pointed to alignments.

We stomped on through this vast Bronze Age geometry puzzle, alignments

It looked like a huge squatting bird.

A stone shaped like a triangular pyramid.

Some were shaved down one side as if to provide a sight line.

Water-gathering basins carved out of the rock pointed to alignments.

Bronze Age grave at the North End.

Big Atlantic breakers smashed on the rocks below.

Moorland gave way to cliffs.

everywhere, and looked forward to coming back to decipher this enigma that had been written so large on the plateau.

Finally we reached the end of the island. Moorland gave way to cliffs. The sea rolled in, big Atlantic breakers that smashed on the rocks below. We found a soft mattress of heather behind a rock out of the wind and watched and listened to the power of it all.

Above, seagulls hung in the breeze, lazily finding a thermal, flicking a feather, dipping a wing and rising upwards effortlessly. They watched everything, particularly looking for any shoals of fish. Suddenly they'd get bored, let the wind catch them and be swept off down the island.

Out of the wind, the sun was warm and we lay back, squinting at the blue sky, the crash of waves in our ears and absolutely nothing going on in our brains. This was real relaxation, as we slumbered at the edge of the world.

We were sleeping among many from the Bronze Age who lay there. Next to us a Bronze Age tomb marked the landscape – one of many. What mysteries lay around us? We drifted off into that wonderful netherworld between wakefulness and sleep, cradled on the soft moss at the most ancient and unspoilt part of the island. It was the start of our stay on a magical island, and the beginning of a journey of discovery that would reveal an astonishing history and plenty of sweet food for the imagination.

CHAPTER TWO

SHIPWRECK!

There have been more shipwrecks on Scilly than on any other group of islands in the world – around 530 are chronicled, but the real total may be nearer 900.

From the middle of the 19th century onwards most were photographed by the Gibson family. Many sailors drew their last breath in the sea around Scilly after their vessels had fallen amongst the jagged granite.

Traditionally, Scillonians treated shipwrecked sailors as their own, risking their lives on countless occasions to try and save strangers who might be out there among the rocks, crashing seas and howling wind.

Disorientating fog was often the cause of wrecks. Occasionally smaller boats were lucky and might ground gently before easing off again on the next tide. Even the *Scillonian* suffered this fate. But for most seamen a shipwreck on Scilly was a desperate and deadly business.

The following photographs are reproduced by kind permission of the Gibson family.

The Gue Longie.

The gig Czar *on the way to the wreck of the* Minnehaha.

SHIPWRECKS ON SCILLY PHOTOGRAPHED BY THE GIBSON FAMILY

Reginald.

King Cadwallon.

Pasteur.

Scillonian.

Horsa.

Earl of Arran.

Plympton.

CHAPTER THREE

HOW SCILLY NEARLY BECAME A DOCKYARD

Situated at the gateway to the English Channel, the Isles of Scilly's naval history over the last two centuries is a curious story of what-might-have-been. Geographically, Scilly sits in a vital and strategic location – and for two centuries the islands featured strongly in government plans for the defence of the realm.

This photograph of 1870, taken at the time of the Franco-Prussian War, shows the German fleet sheltering in St Mary's Roads after a storm.

A map drawn in 1810, and attached to the report proposing Scilly as a naval dockyard, shows Scilly's strategic importance to the defence of Britain.

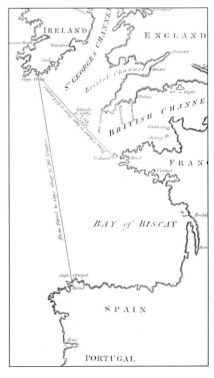

In the 18th century, and at the beginning of the 19th, a serious problem for the Royal Navy was the location of their main naval ports. The Royal Navy could take days, sometimes weeks, to tack their square-rigged sailing ships down Channel from their bases in Portsmouth or Chatham against the prevailing sou'westerlies.

By the time they reached the Western Approaches, it might be too late to cut off a Spanish or French fleet coming up from Biscay. On the way, ships could become scattered or wrecked in high winds, and the alternative – keeping them at sea – required constant refreshment of water and victuals.

The Isles of Scilly, conveniently positioned in the Western Approaches to the Channel looked like an ideal place to base a fleet, positioning them right where they were needed.

In 1776, when Britain went to war against the British rebels in the colonies in North America, the Admiralty became painfully aware that they had little or no proper charts of the eastern seaboard of America. In fact, if truth were known, they had very few proper charts of anywhere. Each year, for every ship that they lost in action they lost nine from running aground. Something had to be done.

Captain Cook.

Alexander Dalrymple.

A: A massive breakwater drawn from Samson, rather clumsily rubbed out and re-drawn.

B: Breakwater from Gugh designed to narrow the channel.

The Dalrymple chart, altered by the Lords of the Admiralty.

To deal with the chart problem of the American Revolutionary War, their Lordships commissioned The Atlantic Neptune – a secret series of surveys and charts of the American coastline – the first truly accurate mapping of that continent's shores and harbours.

A few years later, it was decided to create a 'Hydrographical Office' where all available charts and maps could be gathered together under one roof. It would be nothing less than the nation's most valuable intelligence resource. But first they needed a 'Hydrographer to the Navy', someone who could set up this major programme, and who had the experience and ability to pull it all together.

The first and obvious choice was Captain James Cook who had already discovered and charted more parts of the world than any other man. However, to their Lordships' dismay, Captain Cook had left on his third and last great expedition to try and discover a northern passage linking the Pacific to the Atlantic – a voyage that would lead to his tragic death in Hawaii three years later.

Unable to contact Cook, their Lordships fell back on their second choice – Alexander Dalrymple.

Dalrymple was nearly as famous and remarkable as Cook. He had explored extensively through the southern oceans and was Hydrographer to the mighty East India Company. Captain Cook had used many Dalrymple charts on his voyages.

Their Lordships were a demanding group of men. They insisted that Dalrymple prove his suitability for the task of Hydrographer to the Navy by producing a test chart. The area they asked him to chart was the Isles of Scilly. It had already been surveyed by Graham Spence in his remarkable 'Survey of the Scilly Isles' of 1792, and now they asked Dalrymple to show his worth by producing a workable chart based on this earlier survey data. It was, in essence, a drawing test.

Swallowing his pride, Dalrymple did as he was asked and produced the chart. Their Lordships were well satisfied and he was given the job – thus becoming

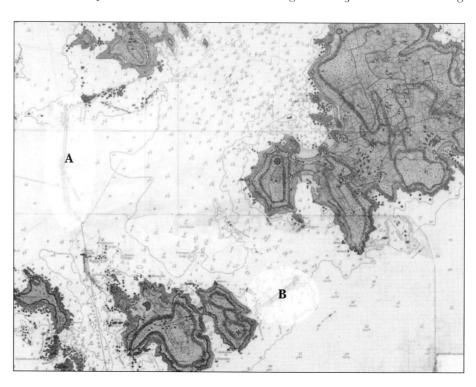

the first Hydrographer to the Navy and the founder of the United Kingdom Hydrographic Office, which to this day still produces 65% of all modern charts in the world. Admiralty charts remain a byword for accuracy and legibility and are a Great British success story.

As the new 19th century began their Lordships were still toying with the idea of basing a Home Fleet in Scilly. It all seemed so logical.

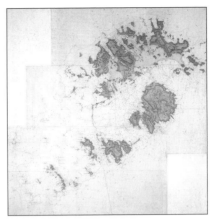

The complete Dalrymple chart of Scilly.

Sometime around 1802 they decided to do something about it. They called for Dalrymple's chart of Scilly – the one that he had produced as his exam. It was still lodged in Whitehall. They blew the dust off it, spread it out and looked at the problem from above, as it were. It seemed perfectly straightforward, they could build extra breakwaters (moles) – the islands themselves to some extent would provide a further natural breakwater – and the fleet could shelter there and be watered and victualled before setting out on voyages. Building materials would not be a problem, the islands were made of granite weren't they? So they got out their pencils...

They first drew a breakwater from Gugh (part of St Agnes) that was designed to narrow the channel between St Mary's and St Agnes – one of the main entrances to the anchorage. Any ship that approached from this side would then have to pass right under the guns of Star Castle. A second even more massive breakwater was drawn from Samson and pointing towards the other side of St Agnes. After some consideration, this was rather clumsily rubbed out and re-drawn.

On paper, scrawled over Dalrymple's immaculate chart, their Lordships had created what looked like a safe sheltered anchorage with breakwaters to add further protection. Guns positioned at Star Castle would provide defensive protection. Now all they needed was to appoint someone to take charge and turn their ideas for Scilly into reality. The poisoned chalice was passed to Benjamin Tucker, Surveyor-General of the Duchy of Cornwall.

In 1810 his report was published – *The Report of The Surveyor-General of The Duchy of Cornwall to His Royal Highness The Prince of Wales concerning The Obstacles, Facilities and Expence attending The Formation of A Safe and Capacious Roadstead with The Islands of Scilly.* After a lengthy preamble apparently designed to appeal to the Prince of Wales' vanity, we get to the meat.

The report cover.

First comes an appended report from Humphrey Davy dated 1808 that attests to the satisfactory analysis of drinking water on Scilly. According to Davy the water contained '1/1000 of its weight of saline matter; and one hundred parts of the saline matter contain:

	Parts
Muriate of soda	70
Of Lime and Magnesia	26
Sulphur of Lime	3
Carbonate	1

'The water is not brackish; any subterranean communication with the sea would occasion the presence of a much larger quantity of saline matter, for in that part of the Ocean the salt water contains about 1/32 of saline matter.

'A part of the marine salt which exists in small quantities in the water of Trusco (sic) may possibly be conveyed in the spray of the sea; but there is no reason why it may not be a native impregnation of the spring that feeds the lake.

'I cannot conceive that the water can be improper or unhealthy for common use, or that it can be injured in a voyage.'

St Mary's Harbour and Roadstead in 1875, with the mackerel fleet in port.

With the vital question of the suitability of the drinking water now answered, next came a question-and-answer session designed to establish whether or not Scilly could ever make a safe harbour.

The three most experienced Scilly Pilots were invited to Exeter where they were interrogated. They were described by Mr Tyrwhitt of Scilly as being 'esteemed as the most intelligent and best Pilots for these islands'. They were Thomas Mortimer with 40 years' experience, James Duff with 25 years' experience, and John Jenkin with 20 years' experience. Only Mortimer could sign his name, the other two signing with a cross.

Posing the questions were Mr Benjamin Tucker himself, aided by 'Captain Edward Marsh, Royal Navy, commanding the Sea Fencibles upon the islands; and Mr John Johns, Steward of the Islands, and Lieutenant of the Veteran Battalion'.

Some of their answers will interest sailors today. For example, which winds occasion the greatest sea and danger, and are most to be guarded against in St Mary's Roadstead?

'From SW to WSW. When the wind gets more to the westward, the water begins to smoothen, as the Nundeeps and Crim break off the Sea; and when the wind is more to the southward, the sea is broken off by Annette, and the Western Rocks'.

'The greatest sea sets from SW, even with the wind at WSW.'

Asked at what time of tide ships in the Roads ride the hardest, the Pilots replied: 'With the wind to the westward they ride hardest with the flood; and with the ebb with an easterly wind'.

Tucker showed them their Lordships' sketches on the charts and asked the Pilots for their views. Carefully he described the proposal so that there could be no mistake.

'Supposing that a breakwater, above the surface at high water spring tides, should be made to the shoal ground south of the Monalter Ledges, from thence towards the rocks called Bristolman's Ledge, as shewn on the Chart; and also a breakwater from the Round Rock to the Spanish Ledge in St Mary's Sound, what effect would they have upon the anchorage, and what degree of safety would be derived therefrom?'

The Pilots' answer was precise and suspiciously brief. Without any qualification they apparently answered: 'It would be a safe and secure anchorage in all winds and weathers.'

After answering various innocuous questions, they were then asked 'If the breakwaters in Broad Sound and St Mary's Sound are made, with what wind could ships of the line be carried to sea from the Roadstead?' The answer was once again short and simple: 'With any wind, unless it blew so hard that they could not carry sail'.

Next to testify, with a report appended to the main document, was John Rennie of London who writes like a civil engineer. He had never been to Scilly but proposed the construction of a mole in Broad Sound and another in St Mary's Sound to shelter the Roadstead for ships of war and merchantmen. He proposed each mole to be eighty feet high, built in the sea where the average depth is ten fathoms. One would be nearly a mile long running between 'Great Smith and the little Minalto passing over the Scar'. The cost of this would be an incredible £1,690,000 – an astronomical sum for those days.

Rennie continues 'If St Mary's Sound is left open, a great sea would tumble in from the South; and therefore to shelter this Sound and to allow a free entrance for shipping a mole will be required from Gugh island to the eastern edge of the Spanish Ledge a distance of one thousand yards, where the water is, generally speaking four fathoms deep... this mole, I apprehend, will cost at least three hundred and twenty thousand pounds, which being added to the former, makes a total amount of two million and ten thousand pounds'.

The next section of the main Report contains Daniel Alexander and James Greig's *Survey Proposing Means to form a Roadstead for Men of War in the Islands of Scilly*. The two gentlemen came down from London pausing only in Exeter to be present at the interrogation of the Scilly Pilots. They brought with them copies of Graeme Spence's 1792 *Survey of the Scilly Isles*. This was the splendidly accurate Survey that had taken the young Spence 3 years to produce, during which time he had been rowed round the islands to make his observations from a gig. The Spence Survey also included the first accurate measurements of the tidal currents.

Alexander and Greig's Survey rejects any idea of building a breakwater out from Samson, similarly they reject proposals to link Samson to the Minalto rocks since neither of the constructions would provide sufficient shelter.

Instead they proposed two breakwaters: one would run from the Scar to Bristolman's Ledge, providing shelter from prevailing SW and WSW winds while leaving a NW and SW passage for shipping at either end. The second breakwater would join Spanish Ledge to Gugh sheltering the Roadstead from the SE and S gales.

Detail showing Bristolman's Ledge.

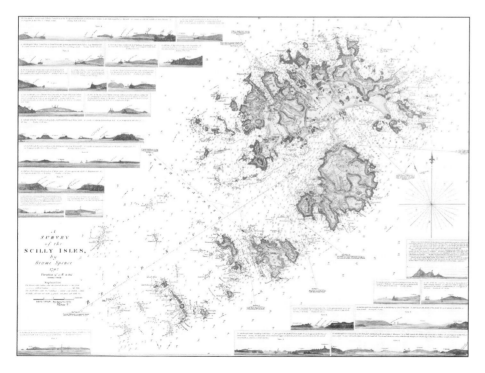

Graeme Spence's 1792 Survey of the Scilly Isles.

'The Roadstead so formed... would contain about four-fifths of a square mile, and accommodate about nine sail of the line, with room for getting under weigh in blowing water, and also room to the NE for frigates and ships of less draft of water; and we take the liberty to add, that in our opinion no other Roadstead can be formed in Scilly.'

But how to build this major civil engineering project? 'Before we went to the Islands, we had been informed by masons, etc that the whole Islands were a congeries of uninterrupted granite. We find this not to be so....'

What Alexander and Greig had discovered was that Scilly consists of outcrops of granite rather than being solid rock. Their original thought that the islands themselves could be quarried and the stone run down to jetties on a railway now seemed impractical. While they could see many great boulders around the shores of the islands where they had become detached from the soil by storms, Alexander and Greig were uncertain as to how much suitable rock lay underground ready to be quarried. Nonetheless they applied themselves to describing how the breakwaters were to be built.

The breakwaters 'should be formed of rough irregular shaped (quartoze) blocks of various sizes, from a ton to as great a weight as can well be thrown promiscuously overboard, so as in sinking to jam and find their own beds; having a few smaller intermixed at times to fill interstices'. They proposed buoying the area to be filled and described exact proportions as to width, slope etc.

'It would be advisable to sink one weed with the stone, to induce a growth amongst it, as the work proceeds, as also in calm weather to throw in any kind of shellfish. We had hoped that oysters would have lived here, but we find there are none known in Scilly'.

Next, they calculated the amount of stone required: 'a total of four million seven hundred and thirty thousand and forty tons to be procured and thrown overboard.'

They then studied Captain Marsh's logbook for the previous two years, and concluded 'It appears that the winds in the westerly points occupy half the year, and the situation proposed of the work is in the points where this bad weather reigns, and whose effect these works are intended to overcome, so that we do not think it safe to rely upon more than four months, or one hundred and twenty working days in the year.'

They suggested that a special type of boat be designed and built for the purpose of shifting the rock – 'of thirty tons measurement, fifty tons burthen'. They worked out that 200 of these vessels would be required. Each boat would have a crew of three, and at least 1,300 quarrymen would be required – a total workforce of 1,900 men. The cost of the job would be £1.35 million and it would take five years to complete.

Alexander and Greig sign off with the following: 'It behoves us to observe that great difference of opinion may exist in regard to the cost of a ton of stone, so procured, carried off, and thrown down; but in answer, we beg to remark, that the diminution of the cost will depend much on the facilities which may be given by mechanical means; and by a selection of the proper class of workmen to be employed thereupon.

'It has occurred to us, that as the greatest number will be required on shore that considerable advantage might accrue to this particular work, as well as to the kingdom at large, if convicts were employed, intermingling them in gangs with Cornish miners, and with Navigators (a sort of man in the habit of rock and other work relative to inland-canals)...'

In effect their Report proposed turning Scilly into a convict settlement, where gangs of men would toil at destroying the very islands themselves – dismantling them rock by rock and throwing them into the sea. After five years of this, a naval supply station would be created around an extended Star Castle. Virtually nothing of what we enjoy today would exist.

Alexander and Greig added what was in effect a postscript to their Report: 'Before we close the subject, we beg leave to recommend a very obvious improvement of the Tide Harbour of St Mary's that of joining Rat Island with the Main'. This point would not be overlooked a few years later when a young man from Hertfordshire called Augustus Smith leased the Isles of Scilly from the Duchy of Cornwall in 1834.

Meanwhile, their Lordships puzzled over the Report. It was clear that Scilly could in theory be made into a sheltered Roadstead for a Home Fleet, but at a gigantic cost in terms of both money and labour. Could it possibly be worth it? In the end they did nothing, and as sometimes happens, that was the right decision. Within a few years the problem of where to shelter a sailing fleet would be solved without anyone bringing over any convicts or building a single breakwater.

In 1805, Horatio Lord Nelson defeated the French and Spanish Fleet off the SW coast finally putting to an end Napoleon's hopes of invading England and Ireland. In 1815 he was defeated at Waterloo and banished to Elba. Their Lordships' main enemy finally died in 1821. Once again the idea of Scilly as a naval base could be put on hold.

However, three years before Waterloo, in 1812, an even more significant event took place, in Scotland. A Scots engineer called Henry Bell, inspired by reports of steam-driven river ferries in America, built his steam-powered *Comet* for a ferry service between Glasgow and Greenock on the Clyde. By 1816 the first Channel passenger ferry powered by steam was in operation. The Age of Steam had arrived, and with it came the solution to their Lordships' problem.

By 1834, there seemed little likelihood that Scilly would be needed as a base for sailing ships since the Royal Navy would, in future, be changing to steam ships. With no definite prospect of seeing his land used for a mighty naval base, the Prince of Wales instructed the Duchy of Cornwall to offer the lease of Scilly. It was taken up by the charismatic young man from Hertfordshire – Augustus Smith – heir to a banking fortune, and with a head full of the utilitarian principles of Jeremy Bentham.

He became Scilly's most enduring influence – the Lord Proprietor who would change everything. Instead of a convict island, and a naval base built with stones torn from the islands, he envisaged a Garden of Eden around which would live happy and contented people, gainfully employed and properly educated. His contemporaries thought he was mad.

Meanwhile the Navy's best brains, and their Lordships themselves, were still arguing as to whether steam really was the future, or whether sail should retain a place as propulsion for warships.

Although Augustus Smith now held the lease on Scilly, the plans for the naval base were still pored over in Whitehall. There were those who had not given up on the idea.

Comet.

In 1843 Brunel's Steam Ship *Great Britain* was launched and finally, just two years later, the Royal Navy committed to the technology of the future by ordering seven steam-powered screw-driven warships. No longer would they have to worry about a sailing fleet taking weeks to tack down-Channel to meet the enemy.

Victorian Islanders.

However, for some, the Steam Age was perceived as an irrelevance and their insistence that sail would always be needed meant that the plans for turning Scilly into a naval base were still not thrown away. It was as late as the early 20th century before the idea was finally abandoned. The Navy's new weapon – the Dreadnought battleship – was unveiled in 1905 and instantly made all other battleships obsolete. Dreadnoughts drew too much water to use Scilly as a base, and Admiral Fisher had to look elsewhere for a naval station, and settled on Scapa Flow.

Finally, Scilly really was safe. Or was it?

Within a decade Europe was plunged into the Great War, and Man's ingenuity created new technology and new ways of killing people. A key weapon would be the submersible warship – the submarine. To counter it came the airship and the seaplane.

Now, if you were going to place a squadron of seaplanes to attack submarines that were sinking your ships in the Western Approaches, where would you station them?

The Isles of Scilly, of course, and this time it was Tresco that would be required by the Navy as an important seaplane base.

This time, their Lordships never hesitated for a second...

HMS *Alexandra, 1877.*

To Sail through Smith Sound, keep Castle Bryer A just open to the Right of Great Smith B as it appears in this View of Smith Sound. Bearing N.b.W.true. But observe, when near Upper Quoin Rocks, Castle Bryer must be Opened to the Left of Great Smith, in order to avoid the Quoins.

View 5

A View taken from Graeme Spence's Survey of the Scilly Isles, 1792.

CHAPTER FOUR
AUGUSTUS SMITH 1804–1872
Proprietor from 1834

AUGUSTUS SMITH – PEOPLE'S CHAMPION

Augustus Smith was born in 1804 and died in 1872. Thus he lived through an era when new ideas of social reform, economics and politics were meat and drink to any European or American of intellect and imagination.

Just two decades before Smith was born, the new republic of America formed itself after the Revolutionary War of 1776. Their new Constitution and system of government were created by some of the finest intellects in Christendom. Not just Americans contributed to it. At the end of the 18th century both Edinburgh and Paris – to take two examples – were hotbeds of radical thought, where men gathered to push the boundaries of democratic and social theory.

The Scottish in particular were close to the Founding Fathers, and were hugely influential. The link between these social theorists, with their anxiety to test ideas that might better Man's state, was often Freemasonry. A modern dollar bill carries the Masonic symbolism – there for anyone who looks for it.

Augustus Smith had estates in Hertfordshire and a fortune from the Smith banking empire. After Harrow and Christ Church, Oxford he discovered the works of the social reformer Jeremy Bentham. It was Bentham who declared the objective of all conduct and legislation to be 'the greatest good for the greatest number'. Also, Bentham was passionately interested both in prisons and schools. Education would be an area on which Smith too would leave his mark.

Initially, Smith tried out Bentham's liberal theories of education and employment on his estate in Hertfordshire. It wasn't long before his neighbours took violent exception to what they saw as a reckless assault on the comfortable status quo, and soon Smith was looking for somewhere else where he could put his theories into practice without upsetting the neighbours.

When the Prince of Wales was unable to develop Scilly as a naval base, Smith jumped in and took over a lease for all the islands. His nearest neighbour would now be 30 miles away across some lumpy sea. The hat of Lord Proprietor fitted him perfectly.

Smith had by now embraced Freemasonry, having found little to satisfy him in the established church in Hertfordshire that had publicly denounced his ideas from the pulpit. As a Mason he was plugged into a conduit of radical ideas that flowed through this connection.

He set to work with a will on Scilly, which was not always appreciated by the anarchic islanders. The islands had fallen on hard times, but Scillonians were used to looking out for themselves. After all, no one else had ever helped them before. Their established trades were pilotage of sailing ships that put in for restocking, and a limited amount of fishing and smuggling.

Augustus Smith.

Smugglers' Cottage at the time of Augustus Smith.

The renovated cottage is now a popular holiday retreat.

Islanders on the streets of St Mary's in 1875.

Boatmen John Woodward, Horatio Jenkins, Walter Jenkins and Sam Jenkins

As we have seen, their Lordships had decided against Scilly as a naval base for a sailing fleet once steam made the requirement redundant. For the same reason, the pilot's trade was looking like a bear market. Fewer and fewer ships needed to put into Scilly. However, Smith remembered Alexander and Greig's postscript to their Report and he joined Rat Island to St Mary's and created a quay in order to attract larger ships to a safe and commercial haven. The benefits were immediate – for Pilots, shipwrights, dockers and suppliers of produce such as farmers and small-holders.

Landing the fish, 1875.

Augustus Smith greatly admired the pilots and the boatmen of Scilly, men who were fine seamen and who enjoyed a close camaraderie.

Soon Smith's dictatorial methods were reaping benefits. Better housing was built, youngsters were trained for the merchant marine, and a total of more than sixty trades were established. He never forgot Bentham's principles and emphasis on schooling. Smith established Britain's first compulsory education programme for his tenants – one penny a week to attend school, two pennies if you didn't.

It wasn't long before Augustus Smith realised that Tresco offered him more privacy to develop the kind of property that was suitable for a Lord

Old Grimsby, 1875.

Proprietor. He moved to the island from St Mary's and started to spend his fortune on building a house and garden that would be the envy of his friends, and earn him the nickname 'Emperor'.

He called the house Tresco Abbey, since it stood near the remains of the old St Nicholas Priory.

Tresco Abbey in the 19th century.

The ruined arch of St Nicholas Priory.

In the quarry, from which he took his building stone, it he planted the Tresco Abbey Garden. The site was well chosen. There was plenty of water from a well, and the quarry gave excellent protection from the wind. He built walls and planted wind-breaks. From around the world came plants brought back by seamen who had once lived on Scilly, and knew what he wanted. He established links with Kew through Sir William Hooker, and traded plants with many other great Victorian plant-collectors.

Gardeners and aloes in the Gardens.

A Victorian picnic at the entrance to Piper's Hole on Tresco. This is a cave that contains a subterranean lake on which a boat used to be left to enable visitors to reach a small beach at the far end of the cave.

Augustus Smith (right) and friends.

Soon Tresco Abbey Garden was famous as a place where – thanks to the Gulf Stream – temperate plants could thrive outdoors. Visitors began to come to Tresco. Smith started a collection of ships' figureheads from local wrecks as an additional attraction. Tresco was on the tourist map.

But Smith was famous not just for what he did on Tresco...

Outside Tresco Abbey Garden he had chiseled the message: "All islanders are welcome to walk in these gardens".

Smith not only welcomed visitors to his own grounds, he also fought tenaciously for the public's right to wander in other open spaces. His most famous campaign, the Battle of Berkhamstead Common, became a landmark in conservation history.

While Liberal MP for Truro, Augustus Smith distinguished himself by championing the rights of the public against the claims of the Crown and the Duchy of Cornwall to the ownership of the foreshore on the coast. It is every Briton's birthright to have access to the shoreline, and one that as an island-race we now take for granted. It is one of Augustus Smith's lasting achievements that he made sure this right became enshrined in law.

In 1865 Britain's oldest conservation body The Commons, Open Spaces and Footpaths Society was created to ensure every Briton's rights to walk on common land. Just twelve months later it faced its first serious challenge – from Lord Brownlow of Ashridge. His Lordship decided unilaterally to fence off Berkhamstead Common in order to keep the common man out.

Augustus Smith at the age of 62 took up the cudgel on behalf of the Society against his former neighbour – a powerful and well-known aristocrat. Smith championed the cause of the public's freedom to roam on common land despite his busy political life and deep involvement with his beloved Tresco and the new Garden there. Once again, a basic right of the British people that had been enshrined since before Saxon times was under threat and he was not a man to stand by and let that happen.

A young Augustus Smith in his garden.

Augustus Smith reckoned that if one man could unilaterally fence off common land, then it was reasonable for another unilaterally to un-fence it. He therefore recruited a team of navvies and commissioned two contractors to oversee them. They would be sent by rail to Tring and then to Berkhampstead Common to dismantle Lord Brownlow's two miles of park fencing under the cover of darkness.

The two contractors met at a pub near Euston Station with the intention of catching the train to Tring. They discussed their strategy in much detail over plenty of strong ale, before rolling out of the pub to discover that they had missed the last train.

Meanwhile a team of 120 navvies arrived at Tring station in the middle of the night without a leader. Fortunately, a legal clerk had been sent down by the Solicitor of the Commons Society to observe proceedings. Showing great initiative he cast aside his stiff collar, rolled up his sleeves and took charge of his small army.

He marched his men three miles to the Common, split them into working parties of twelve, and gave them tools and instructions.

By daybreak on that March morning in 1866 two miles of fencing had been neatly laid on the ground, and the navvies marched back to Tring to catch the milk train into London.

Augustus Smith.

Augustus Smith at work in his study.

A view of Old Grimsby in 1875, and a similar view taken in 2002.

Cottages at Back Lane, now demolished.

Row of cottages at Greenside, now part demolished. What was the obelisk?

Four years of a famous legal battle followed before the Berkhamstead Common affair eventually resolved itself in a famous victory for the Commons Society and Augustus Smith. It became a model and inspiration for all the conservation bodies that have followed.

Augustus Smith is justly famous for his incredible Garden at Tresco Abbey, and for creating the dynasty that has continued his work on the island. If one considers the 5,500 years of human occupation on Scilly as a day, then he arrived about three-quarters of an hour before midnight. Yet no other man left such an indelible mark on Scilly.

He had created an extraordinary and successful community on Scilly. He was not often thanked for it. It was his genius to discover and apply the paradox of feudalism: if one man owns everything, then no one else can own anything. Thus, since no one owns anything an equal and classless society is created that avoids the divisive cancer of consumerism. There are two important provisos; it can only work in a small community, and it relies on trust: that the 'Emperor' is benevolent, and that the employees are loyal.

His experiment is unlikely to be repeated elsewhere in Britain, but it is a measure of its lasting success that every year hundreds come to Tresco to share for a short while the benefits of a way of life that disappeared long ago on the mainland.

Three years after his victory in the battle of Berkhamstead Common he was dead, aged 68. He died in Plymouth on his way back to Tresco. He never forgave the Duchy for their arrogance in the battles that he had with them over access to the foreshore. He refused to be buried on any Duchy land – and that included Tresco – so he was interred at St Buryan in Cornwall in a graveyard where, on a clear day, you can just see Scilly. Curiously, his hero Jeremy Bentham also held firm ideas about where his body should lie. His clothed skeleton is on public view in University College, London, which he founded.

Augustus Smith never married, and never expected that his closest relative – nephew Thomas – would have the inclination or means to take the islands on. As a result he bequeathed the agreement back to the Duchy of Cornwall provided they bought it back on his terms. They refused to accept it.

Dolphin Town and Old Grimsby, 1875, showing the old church and the old road.

CHAPTER FIVE
SHIPWRECK! – THE *DELAWARE*

Six months before Augustus Smith died in Plymouth, a shipwreck and rescue took place on Scilly that remains an inspiration to all who sail in these waters.

Augustus Smith was very close to the pilots of Scilly whom he admired for their character and professionalism. He was on the mainland when this incident happened, and died shortly afterwards. This is possibly why the story of the *Delaware* never had the publicity that it deserved, and is little known outside Scilly.

The men involved – almost the entire male population of Bryher – put their lives at risk in a heroic attempt to save others in horrendous conditions a few days before Christmas. No one ever thanked them, no one ever acknowledged what they had done, and no one rewarded them.

This is the story of the *Delaware*.

She was considered a large vessel for her time – an iron steamship of 3,243 tons, built in 1865, but also rigged for sail. On 18 December 1871, exactly a week before Christmas Day, she left Liverpool bound for Calcutta with a cargo of cotton, silks, sheet lead and tin. She had a crew of 44 men.

The Bryher pilots first caught sight of her two days later on 20 December. A strong nor'westerly gale had grown to storm force. It was savage weather. In the huge streaky Atlantic rollers, now breaking into foam, the pilots could see the *Delaware* fighting for her life off Bryher, beyond Hell Bay. She was being pushed towards the Norrard Rocks and Tearing Ledge. If she hit there, her fate would be sealed.

The Bryher men raced to the summit of South Hill with telescopes to get a better view of the impending disaster. To their great distress they could only watch helplessly.

Augustus Smith and pilots from St Agnes.

Looking out from Bryher across Hell Bay in 1875. The Delaware *was lost just out of the photo to the left.*

On board the *Delaware* all the 44 crew fought frantically to save the ship. The engines were red-hot as they tried to force maximum power from the screw. Eventually – and fatally – the engines had to be stopped before they exploded under the pressure.

Without any power from the engines the captain immediately ordered a jib-sail to be hoisted in an attempt to guide the ship between Mincarlo and the other rocks.

If he could just get the ship to run before the wind she would avoid the reef and come inside Mincarlo to calmer waters...

To the despair of the crew, and those on the shore, the jib-sail was carried away by the gale within a few minutes. The remnants of the canvas cracked like a whip in the rigging, as they desperately struggled to raise a stay-sail – their last hope. No sooner had they raised it than it too was swept away in tattered shreds.

The seas were now mountainous – rising up like the sides of houses, with foam being whipped off their crests in the screaming gale. Without power, either from her engines or the sails, the *Delaware* started to wallow broadside-on in the swell, one second in the trough of the waves the next lurching to the crest, being lifted up like a toy in the bath. The poor souls on board could now only commit themselves to the Almighty.

Then a huge sea completely enveloped her and she disappeared under a wall of water. When she reappeared, the horrified onlookers could see that all of the superstructure had been ripped away by the jagged rocks over which she had rolled. She was now a naked hull. The next sea broke over her – and she disappeared forever. No human eye ever saw her again. An iron steamship had vanished within a few seconds on the deadly Norrard Rocks.

A RESCUE PLAN IS CONTRIVED

The Bryher men quickly calculated that if anyone had survived then they might be carried on wreckage towards White Island – a small uninhabited island of about two acres, fairly flat, covered by long grass and sea pinks, with a rocky shore and a boulder-strewn beach. It is situated a quarter-of-a-mile west of Samson, the largest uninhabited island of Scilly.

The onlookers scanned the boiling white seas through telescopes. To their amazement, survivors were spotted – two men clung to half a lifeboat, two gripped a spar, and another hung onto a piece of wreckage.

Five men were still alive from the crew of 44 that had set out together from Liverpool just two days earlier. The Bryher men never hesitated – a rescue plan was swiftly contrived which the pilots among them considered feasible. It was a brave and ambitious plan.

They chose the best sea-boat they had – the six-oared pilot gig *Albion* with a beam of 5ft 6in and 30ft long. The plan was to carry the gig for half-a-mile overland to Rushy Bay where she could be launched with a following wind and sea.

The Scillonian pilot gigs were originally used to row pilots out to sailing ships that wanted to visit the islands. Pilots were essential since the rocks around Scilly were so dangerous to sailing ships, and it was not until the 19th century that accurate charts became readily available to sea captains.

The gigs were built for speed and seaworthiness. The first gig to the ship got the job. Gigs were often owned by syndicates of pilots, and on a good day would drop off more than one pilot before rowing home.

These are modern pictures of gig racing on Scilly. The boats used in the rescue of the survivors of the Delaware were identical. In these pictures, the sea is relatively calm, quite unlike the horrendous gales faced by the Bryher men.

John Jenkins Snr.

Thomas Bickford in later life.

Patrick Trevellick.

The tradition of the gigs is still kept alive today in the weekly rowing races between islands, and the World Championship held in Scilly every May.

The men raced to the gig shed at Great Par. Six oars were lashed across the gig, twelve men took the weight in the crook of their elbow, with their other hand on the gunwhale to steady her. Each one struggled with the pain and the weight, but none complained and none would drop the load while there were still souls to be saved.

THE CREW ARE SELECTED

When they reached Rushy Bay, ten men were selected to make the rescue mission. Their ages ranged from 21 to 50. The names of those heroes were: Patrick Trevellick, William Woodcock, James Jenkins snr, John Jacob Jenkins, Richard Ellis, William Jenkins, Stephen Woodcock, Thomas Bickford, John Webber, Sampson Jenkins.

Their acknowledged leaders were coxswain Patrick Trevellick who took charge of the yoke lines in the gig, and Richard Ellis who was to be dropped on Samson to signal back to Bryher where another crew waited with a sister gig, *March*.

They launched *Albion* and the crew pulled hard as Trevellick steered out into the stormy seas. Pilot gigs are designed to run before huge seas, but the ¼in planks twisted and groaned as they gradually edged towards Samson with every powerful stroke.

They finally made the lea of North Hill and were able to beach. Some of the crew scrambled ashore and dashed to the summit.

THE SURVIVORS' STRUGGLE FOR LIFE

Through their telescopes they could make out the two men on the half-boat being swept towards the rocks of White Island, a quarter-of-a-mile away.

As the half-boat struck the rocks one man jumped into the sea and clung on with his arms. When the backwash left him high and dry he scrambled over the rocks to the grassy shore. The second man stayed on the boat, was then washed up into the rocks and was able to follow his crew-mate to safety.

The two men on the spar were cast ashore about 100 yards further out on the point of the island that is covered at high tide. They were seen to get onto the rocks, but despite a desperate struggle were soon swept off, sucked away by the current and drowned.

The fifth man, on the piece of wreckage, was swept ashore where the two survivors landed. But he had no strength left to get off the rocky beach, and was soon swept away, never to be seen again.

The handful of watchers on the summit could see no other survivors, but from their vantage point were able to see how the two men might be rescued. It would involve rowing the *Albion* further down Samson and carrying her – yet again – across a 200 yard isthmus and re-launching her on the other side.

They ran back to their companions. It was decided to carry out the plan, and if they reached White Island, four men would jump out leaving five men on the sweeps to keep her in the shelter of the island. But first, they had to row down Samson, beach her, and carry her over the isthmus. They reached the East Par beach without incident, and then began the herculean task of again lifting and carrying the 30ft gig.

A HERCULEAN TASK

Progress was desperately slow as they stumbled over seaweed, sand, rye grass and scrub. The full force of the gale whipped sand and spray into their faces and eyes. Eventually they reached the bank at the West Par where they faced their most formidable obstacle. The seaweed-covered boulders and stones gave a treacherous foothold, and the gale all but tore the gig from their grasp. They unshipped the slings and each man grabbed hold of a thwart. If they dropped her on a jagged stone, a plank might shatter and the life-saving mission would be over. With a supreme effort they made it over the bank and laid her on the beach, holding her down against the wind.

All was now set for the struggle against the freezing wind and sea. They left Richard Ellis on Samson to signal their progress back to Bryher, and then they started their heroic pull to White Island.

They met the full force of the Atlantic, with the gale almost slap 'on the nose'. The gig flexed and creaked, the men strained every tired sinew to keep her moving toward White Island. The *Albion* stood on end as each roller passed under her, but slowly they made progress until they were halfway there in the savage wind and seas.

John Jacob Jenkins.

THEY FINALLY REACH WHITE ISLAND

The second half somehow seemed easier to all of them, and they finally made a landing against a stony brow on White Island. They watched for the best moment and then ran in quickly on the back of a wave. As the sea receded the four men jumped out as arranged, and on the next wave the *Albion* floated off again without damage.

The youngest man aboard – John Jacob Jenkins – was the first to reach the two survivors. What happened next was pure farce. The two survivors gathered stones and were prepared to throw them to defend themselves against the islanders whom, they had been told, were little better than savages. How wrong they were.

RESCUED, CLOTHED AND COMFORTED

One survivor was without a jacket and in bare feet, the other had no trousers, and both were soaked and freezing. The *Albion* crewmen gave them their own socks, jackets and a blanket. After reassuring them, they then carefully searched the island for more survivors – without success. Eventually the *Albion* returned to the rocky shore, and after lifting the survivors aboard they started the long pull back to Samson – this time with the wind and sea behind them.

Back on Samson, Richard Ellis had signalled for the sister gig, *March*. That crew then repeated their companions' feat of carrying her to Rushy Bay before launching her for Samson.

The *Albion* reached Samson safely, coming ashore on a wave and being hauled up the beach by the exhausted crew. There they left her, while they struggled across the isthmus with the two survivors. At East Par they found a fern rick where they rested for the first time.

When the *March* finally arrived at East Par on Samson the *Albion* crew took her over and fought their way back to Bryher with the survivors. On Bryher they took them to John Jacob Jenkins' cottage 'Southward' where they gave them hot drinks and put them to bed.

The two survivors were the First Mate – a Black man called MacWhinnie – and the Third Mate who had the same name as many of his rescuers – Jenkins. The men left on Samson stayed there all night and carried the Albion back

First Mate, MacWhinnie.

over the isthmus. Next day every man on Bryher helped bring everyone and everything back to Bryher.

Neither gig was ever used again for pilotage. The *March* had been built to beat the *Albion* – which she invariably did – and other rival pilots then built the even-faster *Golden Eagle*. The *Albion* pilots later commissioned *The Czar* – the fastest of all – with an extra oar. *The Albion* was sold to Mr A Watts of St Mary's who used her planking to build a 10ft sailing dinghy. *The March* was allowed to fall to pieces on Bryher.

NEVER ACKNOWLEDGED... BUT NOT FORGOTTEN

Five days after the rescue it was Christmas Day, but the Bryher men who risked their lives in this extraordinary and heroic rescue were never acknowledged, never thanked nor rewarded in any way by any authority.

But at least on Scilly their selfless bravery is remembered and is still looked upon as a glittering example to all who call themselves seamen. If you sail a boat in Scilly then look back over your shoulder into History and tip your hat to better men than us.

Robert Maybee of St Mary's wrote a poem about the rescue. Here are a few verses.

> *And on the bridge the captain stood,*
> *He was a valiant man;*
> *Although his leg was broke, and foot as well,*
> *He still kept in the van*
> *But then an awful sea broke on the ship,*
> *And snapt the bridge in two;*
> *The captain then was swept away,*
> *And near fifty sailors too.*
> *But Bryher men had watched the boat,*
> *And volunteered so brave*
> *That to White Island they would go*
> *The shipwrecked men to save*
> *Those Bryher men stood on the hill*
> *That dark & stormy day;*
> *They manned their boat, and with great speed*
> *For Sampson rowed away.*
>
> *Over Sampson they carried their boat*
> *Crossed lakes and bars of sand*
> *Determined quite to face it all*
> *And bring them safe to land.*
> *They launched their boat down in the sea*
> *And on the foaming billow tost;*
> *Their friends and wives stood weeping at the scene*
> *And thought they must be lost.*
> *Quickly they rowed their boat along,*
> *For staunch was every man*
> *They quickly got the shipwrecked men*
> *And brought them safe to land.*
> *Now may God bless those Bryher men*
> *For all that they have done.*
> *Their deed of daring shall be known*
> *Wherever shines the sun.*

Just 5 years later another shipwreck would take place on Scilly, resulting in terrible loss of life. This time, though, the world's attention would be focused on the islands and the pilots would receive full recognition for their rescue.

CHAPTER SIX
THOMAS ALGERNON SMITH
DORRIEN SMITH 1846–1918

When Augustus Smith died, unmarried, in 1872, his nearest relatives were his brother Robert and his sister Frances. Frances had married Colonel Thomas Le Marchant whose fortune was reputed to have come from privateering in the Channel Islands. But it was to his brother's son – Thomas Algernon Smith Dorrien – that the lease on Scilly was left

Augustus Smith's brother had married Mary Anne Drever, grand-daughter and heiress of Thomas Dorrien, a family of bankers and merchants. In acknowledgement, one supposes, of the origin of their fortune, they added the name Dorrien to their surname – becoming Mr and Mrs Smith Dorrien. This prolific couple then produced 15 children. Thomas Algernon, the eldest boy, and Augustus's nephew, held a commission as a Lieutenant in the Tenth Hussars.

When the Duchy refused to accept back the lease of Scilly offered by Augustus, Thomas Algernon at 26-years-old became the new Lord Proprietor. In accordance with Augustus Smith's wishes that only a Smith inherit the estate on Scilly, Thomas Algernon attached a second and final Smith to his surname, becoming Thomas Algernon Smith Dorrien Smith.

In 1875 he married Edith Tower, daughter of Augustus Smith's close friend and confidante Lady Sophia Tower, but without, on this occasion, feeling it necessary to expand his surname any further.

Thomas Algernon Smith Dorrien Smith.

The New Grimsby-side of the island around the turn of the century.

This photograph shows Mrs Smith Dorrien (née Drever), seated centre and surrounded by her 15 children and other members of the family in 1902. Her husband Robert had already joined the Great Majority.

Her children, in order, were: Thomas Algernon, Frederick, Theophilus, Walter, Arthur, Horace, Frances, Marian, Amy, Edith, Alma, Mary, Maude, Laura and Dora. The fecund Mrs Smith Dorrien spent much of her adult life pregnant. Interestingly, only three of her girls married. Perhaps they were discouraged from doing so, since the dowry payments would have amounted to a small fortune.

Behind her, with the walrus moustache, is Thomas Algernon Smith Dorrien Smith, aged 56, and the Lord Proprietor of Scilly. To her right sits Horace Smith Dorrien – one of the very few survivors of the Zulu slaughter at Isandhlwana and Rorke's Drift. Horace later became a general and a hero of the Great War when he refused to retreat ('The Man who Disobeyed') and held the line against the Germans.

Thomas Algernon was with Baden Powell at Mafeking. When the Boer siege was finally lifted after more than 7 months, Horace Smith Dorrien was among the relieving troops – as also was Baden Powell's brother.

The elderly lady in front of Mrs Drever in the photograph is Augustus Smith's sister Frances Le Marchant – well into her nineties by this time.

The present church was consecrated in 1879 – about the time that these photographs were taken. Compare with the photograph on page 28.

PRIVATEERS to BANKERS – The Dorriens

Let us divert for a moment to look at the Dorriens.

John Dorrien, Mary Anne Drever's great grandfather, had been Chairman of the mighty East India Company in 1760 during the days of Clive. One of his sons then inherited a vast fortune from an uncle – a privateer called Nicholas Magens – that included a mass of silver bullion captured from the French. It was the largest prize ever taken. In gratitude for his inheritance, John Dorrien's son expanded his surname from Dorrien to Magens Dorrien Magens

Cottages in Back Lane, Old Grimsby. These no longer exist.

Privateering was a profitable business. Privateers were licenced pirates who paid a commission to the Crown and in return had permission to loot and pillage foreign ships on the high seas.

Each Monarch in Europe licenced his own privateers. A certain sort of rogue was attracted to the game, and it wasn't long before privateers found ways to cheat their employers.

There also seems to have been an upward mobility to which privateers aspired. Once they had a goodly stash of gold and silver, they became banks and insurance companies. Many of the country's commercial and financial structures appeared to be run by a 'brotherhood' with its roots in piracy.

To counter cheating by his licenced pirates, the King employed Commissioners to watch the coasts and to follow the privateers when they returned. It was not that successful. Particularly when privateers or former privateers were appointed, in a poacher-turned-gamekeeper philosophy. At least one Commissioner was called Dorrien.

The fortune that Magens Dorrien Magens inherited from Nicholas Magens had been acquired under somewhat cloudy circumstances in 1745.

Nicholas Magens had dealings with various French merchants whom he knew had commissioned three ships to sail to South America to pillage for gold and silver.

As a privateer, Nicholas Magens sent his own ships to intercept the French on their return and conveniently met them within a few days of sailing into the Atlantic; the fight was brief and the French ships' hulls were miraculously undamaged by English cannon fire. The French crews – mostly uninjured – were captured, well treated, and then landed in Ireland.

Although a massive amount of treasure – in fact the largest prize ever – reached London safely, complexities involving insurance claims left some people believing that somehow Magens and the French merchants had done rather better out the incident than they should.

However little of this bothered Magens Dorrien Magens who had inherited the remnants of this huge fortune.

In 1794, the Dorrien family bank 'Dorrien, Rucker, Dorrien & Martin' changed its name to 'Dorrien, Magens, Mello & Co'.

Four years later, in 1798, a major financial disaster hit the country, and created one of the most worrying episodes in England's history. We were at war with France, threatened with invasion, prices were high, taxation was astronomical and food supplies were low. In addition there was an acute

Old Grimsby.

shortage of coinage. The price of silver was so high that people melted coin down. Gold and copper coins were also scarce.

With no proper means of trading, everyone was intolerably affected. It was during this crisis, that Gilreay's cartoon showing the Bank of England as a skinny harridan sitting on her treasure chest created forever the Bank's nickname of 'The Old Lady of Threadneedle Street'.

In an attempt to relieve the crisis that shortage of coinage had created, a group of bankers lead by Magens Dorrien Magens sent a vast amount of silver to The Mint to be turned into shillings. The coins were struck but before they could be distributed Prime Minister William Pitt stopped the process and ordered them to be turned back into ingots. It seems to have been a conflict between the City and a Government who resented being up-staged by a group of bustling merchants. However around twenty Dorrien Magens shillings escaped the crucible and are now some of the most sought-after and valuable coins coveted by numismatists.

Eventually, after eighteen months, the Government returned the silver. It had been a disastrous venture for the merchants. The shortage of silver for coins lasted for another twenty years, until 1816, when Prime Minister, Lord Liverpool, solved the problem by replacing silver with gold and creating a new coin – the sovereign – that stayed in circulation until 1914.

New Grimsby.

Thomas Algernon Smith Dorrien Smith arrived on Tresco in 1872 to find that his inheritance – Scilly – had suffered a serious downturn in prosperity.

With no public telegraph system the islands were cut off from the rest of the world; the Steam Age and iron ships had substantially reduced the demand for wooden ships to be built on Scilly. Steam ships avoided coming to St Mary's, preferring the mainland ports like Falmouth, so the pilots' trade had slumped as well. Local fisherman had no easy access to the mainland fish markets, and the market for early potatoes had been undercut by growers in the Channel Islands. Something had to be done.

It was Thomas Algernon who came up with the idea of growing narcissi for the mainland market Scilly had a month's climate advantage over the mainland meaning that the flowers could command a premium price.

By 1886 he was exhibiting 150 different varieties at the St Mary's Flower Show, and had created and organised the trade on Scilly. St Mary's Quay was again enlarged to allow steamers as well as sailing boats from the off-islands to load and unload flowers. It was also of value to the fishermen who needed to get their catch to the mainland. He built glass-houses to bring on the flowers even earlier, thus catching the earliest possible market and getting the maximum from the selling season.

In short, he had achieved a remarkable turn-around in the islands' prosperity.

The Abbey and Gardens in Victorian times.

Augustus Smith's pride and joy – the Abbey Garden – was beginning to mature and under his nephew's direction it began to rank as a serious botanic experiment of international renown. Plants from South Africa and South America were established, and magnificent Monterey pine and cypress were planted successfully.

On an island there is always something to do in a boat, particularly in summer, and Thomas Algernon enjoyed being on the water. Fishing was a favourite pastime, and the waters teemed with fish – far more so than today when the big 4-mile nets scoop up the entire shoal leaving none to breed and grow. Sailing was also a summer activity, although gentlemen were expected to wear a tie whilst at sea – again rather different than today.

The story of how a little paradise was being created on Tresco had reached the ears of the Royal Family, and Queen Victoria visited Scilly. Later in 1902 Thomas Algernon had the honour of receiving King Edward VII, a year after Victoria's death. He arrived in the Royal Yacht *Victoria & Albert*, together with a full naval escort.

Thomas Algernon, sailing. Jacket and tie were de rigeur even when on the water.

The King visits Pulpit Rock, St Mary's.

The King (back to camera) leaves from St Mary's, boarding Thomas Algernon's launch.

Victoria's third son, Prince Arthur, Duke of Connaught, also visited in 1905. The Duke was a distinguished soldier, having been the Commander in Chief in Ireland, and would hold the same position in the Mediterranean before becoming Governor General of Canada.

Royal visits were always an excitement, and a splendid spectacle as the Navy always escorted the Royal Family with their latest and smartest warships.

Thomas Algernon and his family of five daughters and two sons lived on Scilly for more than 40 years. He died in 1918, and the inscription on the family monument reads "He devoted his life unselfishly to these islands and added greatly to their prosperity and beauty".

An annual 'Garden Bazaar' was held in the Gardens for all islanders. This photograph was taken around the turn of the century.

CHAPTER SEVEN
SHIPWRECK! – THE *SCHILLER*

After Thomas Algernon Dorrien Smith and his new wife returned to Tresco from their honeymoon in Paris, in March 1875, they immediately found themselves plunged into a Scillonian tragedy that shocked the world.

The first they knew of it was when a boatload of cold, bedraggled, frightened people were found in a lifeboat in New Grimsby. They had come from the *Schiller*, a modern German transatlantic liner.

Thomas Algernon immediately took charge of operations both on Tresco and on St Mary's.

The story of the *Schiller*'s terrible last voyage became headline news around the world. What made it so tragic and heart-rending was that many of those who lost their lives were women and children.

The German Transatlantic Steam Navigation Company of Hamburg was one of the largest shipping lines in existence when they commissioned an iron screw steamer from Napiers of Glasgow for delivery in August 1873. At 3,421 tons, 380 feet long with a 40 foot beam, the *Schiller* was one of the greatest passenger ships afloat and soon became a popular choice with both German and American passengers.

On 27 April 1875 she loaded in New York before starting a scheduled voyage to Plymouth, Cherbourg, and her home port of Hamburg. Before the passengers embarked, a valuable cargo had to be stored in the holds – sewing machines, agricultural implements, flour, feathers for upholstery, kegs of resin and the Royal Mail's bags of letters and packets from New Zealand and Australia. One very special consignment was delivered under armed guard – 300,000 coins including twenty-dollar gold coins – worth over £6m in today's money.

SS Schiller.

With the cargo safely stowed, the *Schiller* received her passengers – 120 in steerage-class, 75 in second-class and 59 in first-class. Among the latter was Mr Kornblum, a paper manufacturer from New York, who brought with him 85 gold watches, a mass of jewellery and £500 in coin. Another New Yorker was Louise Holzmeister who looked forward to celebrating her 24th birthday in a few days time. Also aboard was champion Cornish wrestler Richard Williams from Chacewater.

There were 254 passengers and 118 crewman when the *Schiller* slipped the pier and set sail from New York for Plymouth.

The *Schiller* made excellent time across the Atlantic, and by 7 May was nearing the Isles of Scilly – well ahead of schedule. At 8 o'clock that evening a thick fog descended. Within fifteen minutes, it was impossible to see the length of the ship.

Captain Thomas immediately took in sail and proceeded at 4 knots under power. An hour later, with the Bishop Light not seen or heard, the Captain asked for volunteers from the male passengers to act as extra lookouts – with the prize of a bottle of Krug champagne to the first man to see the light or hear the fog bell. The prize was never collected. At 10 o'clock that night the *Schiller* struck the Retarrier Ledges. She had managed to pass inside the lighthouse.

The engines were put astern and the fatally damaged *Schiller* pulled clear of the reef, but as she wallowed in the swell three huge waves in succession lifted her up and flung her back on the Ledges – this time broadside on. The dense fog, heavy seas, the darkness, the slippery decks and angle at which she lay combined to magnify the horror of the catastrophe for those on board.

Complete panic broke out among the passengers. Men, women and children rushed to the boats screaming and crying and some of the men drew knives, the better to fight for a place in the life-boats. Captain Thomas fired his revolver in the air to restore discipline. Eventually running out of ammunition, he was obliged to draw his sword to drive out the cowardly men from the 8 life-boats.

Two boats and their occupants were then flattened when the funnel crashed down on them, two others capsized after being cut loose from the painted-up chocks. Another two were smashed against the hull as they were lowered, drowning the occupants. Just two boats got away safely. 320 men, women and children were left aboard to face a night of mounting horror – and a rising tide.

They managed to fire the cannon half a dozen times before the powder got wet, and then rockets were sent up into the blanketing fog.

On nearby St Agnes, a cannon shot was heard but was assumed to be the normal report gun fired by ships as they passed the Bishop. However, a couple of islanders – including pilot Obadiah Hicks – wondered.

The gun was also heard on St Mary's and a routine shipping report was sent to the *Schiller*'s agent in Plymouth.

On board the *Schiller* things were desperate. By midnight she had developed an even heavier list and Captain Thomas ordered all the women and children into the deckhouse structure over the midships saloon. More than fifty huddled there, weeping mothers clutching bewildered, howling children.

At about 2 am, the Captain, the ship's doctor and the Chief Engineer were swept off the bridge by a huge wave that raked the ship from stem to stern. A succession of heavy seas then continued to sweep the ship. One ripped off the deckhouse roof, the next hurled the occupants into the sea. Men would never forget those screams. The women and children who sheltered there were all drowned.

Men started lashing themselves to the rigging, on each of the masts. One iron mast was swept away almost at once, taking all on it under the water. The other mast stayed upright with men clinging to it. A passenger, Mr Percival, urged them higher before having his brains dashed out by a loose chain just as he reached the crow's nest. Another passenger called West used Percival's body as shelter from the thrashing spray and survived to be picked up later from the sea.

On St Agnes, Obadiah Hicks and his crew resolved at first light – 4 am – to take out the gig *O & M* (for Obadiah and Mary) into the huge seas and thick fog to investigate stories from other islanders of more than one cannon shot being heard.

They rowed out past Melledgen and Corrigan, and along the length of the Western Rocks, and as the mist cleared for a moment, they saw to their horror a mast and some sails of a large ship protruding from Retarrier Ledges.

The crew of the *O & M* decided to take the difficult passage through the Neck of Crebawathen, shipping several big seas as they pulled desperately on the sweeps to get nearer to the wreck.

They found the sea littered with debris. Above the pounding surf, they heard the dreadful screams of the men in the rigging and those clinging to wreckage.

Then a huge piece of wreckage smashed the rudder of *O & M* and the danger of fatal damage to her ¼ inch planking meant that Obadiah Hicks had no option but to order his crew to row for St Mary's to raise the alarm. He was able to pluck 5 survivors, including Mr West, from the sea before turning away.

On the way, they alerted two fishing boats from Sennen which were sheltering from the storm and which then went to the wreck. *O & M* reached St Mary's at 7 am, and by 8 am the mail-steamer *Lady of the Isles* was steamed up and took both the St Mary's lifeboat and the *O & M* in tow. The big seas had the steamer's decks completely awash, and eventually the *O & M* had to cut herself free when two of her planks stove in. The gig was lucky to reach land, with the crew bailing frantically to stay afloat.

Mass graves in St Mary's churchyard.

The *Lady of the Isles* found a scene of desolation and horror. The remaining mast by then had fallen, taking those on it to their deaths and nothing could be seen but debris and bodies. Various small boats continued to scour the seas for survivors and a few were found clinging to rocks. The two lifeboats that got away from the *Schiller* when she first hit the Ledges eventually landed on Tresco with 27 people, including the only woman to survive. Of the 355 souls that left New York, just 44 men and one woman survived. No children were saved.

The vast number of bodies presented a problem. Several of the men were recovered stiffened in rigor mortis with their fists clenched as if they had fought a last frantic battle for survival. Several female bodies had to be prised away from the bodies of small children that they were found clutching. All this sadness and horror profoundly affected the islanders, not least the large number of drowned children that were recovered, many of whom appeared angelic and looked strangely peaceful in death.

Some bodies, on the instructions of relatives, were embalmed for return to America in simple black-painted deal coffins, but the majority were buried in three mass graves in St Mary's churchyard. The granite had to be blasted with dynamite to make room for them.

Mr Kornblum perished with his watches, as did Louise Holzmeister whose heart-broken husband erected a fine memorial to her in St Mary's church.

Richard Williams the champion Cornish wrestler survived and was known as "Schiller" Williams ever after. 310 souls – mostly German – were dead and the islanders, led by Mr Dorrien Smith, plunged into the deepest mourning.

Many bodies were disinterred for identification by relatives.

AFTERMATH

The tragedy shocked the world. The practice of sounding a gun to report arrival was abandoned at once. Henceforth, it would only ever be used as a distress signal.

Reporters flocked to cover the story. The kindness, compassion and sensitivity of the islanders won universal praise, as did the honesty of poor Cornish and Scillonian fishermen who handed in thousands of pounds-worth of recovered valuables and jewels.

The funeral in St Mary's.

Many bodies were disinterred after burial for identification by their grieving relatives. A Mr Franz Hauser from Iowa hired divers to find the bodies of his two sisters who perished. One was found held firmly in the clutches of a huge cuttle-fish with tentacles over twelve feet long. Mr Hauser died of shock three days later.

The Emperor and Empress of Germany distributed medallions and bibles to islanders, and gold medals to the coastguard and the lifeboat coxswain. Mrs Dorrien Smith was given a gem-encrusted bracelet with the Empress of Germany's personal thanks for all that the family had done for the survivors

There is an oddly chivalrous epitaph to the story: throughout the two World Wars that followed, it was believed that the German Navy and Luftwaffe had instructions to spare both the Isles of Scilly and the *Scillonian* from attack – on account of kindnesses shown to their countrymen by islanders years before.

A few remnants of the *Schiller* and her cargo survive to this day. The ship's bridge was recovered, and is installed at the Abbey where it does duty as a foot-bridge to a garden annexe. Also in the Abbey is a remarkable piece of angle iron that formed part of the ribs of the *Schiller*. Jammed into it by some massive force is one of the gold 20-dollar coins with which the ship had been laden.

At least one sack of letters was recovered and these were duly delivered by the Royal Mail. Today those postmarked envelopes fetch a tidy sum at auction.

Goods salvaged from the Schiller.

The Schiller *lifeboat.*

The whole morbid episode remained etched in islanders' minds – partly because so many of the *Schiller* victims were children. There were also rumours that a large number of the crew and passengers were drunk that night, having just celebrated an officer's 40th birthday.

Later, the Receiver of Wreck's – a mainlander – was strongly suspected of enriching himself from the proceeds of the valuables, most of which had been turned in by poor Scillonian fishermen.

A letter and envelope rescued from the Schiller.

SOME MAIL GOT THROUGH

Among the several, mail-bags recovered from the wreck ere some on their way from Canada, Australia and New Zealand to London. At least one envelope from those bags has survived.

Mr John Forbes-Nixon wrote to the *Tresco Times*:

> One of my main hobbies is the study and collection of Postal History. As we do so like Scilly I have acquired a few eclectic items relating to them, the major one being a rescued letter that was carried on that fateful journey of the Schiller when she went down on 7 May 1875; it is endorsed in manuscript "This envelope went down in the Sailing Ship Schiller wrecked on a rock of the Scilly Isles in the month of May 1875".
>
> It was from Canada for the Imperial Bank in Lothbury, London and is, of course, a great rarity. I acquired it at auction.

CHAPTER EIGHT
THE EDWARDIAN AGE

To be English and well-born in Edwardian England must have been like winning first prize in the lottery of life. Meanwhile, technology promised to create new vistas and untold wealth for the British Empire and those who lived under the Union flag.

The terrible events that were to come in 1914 didn't cast their shadow back to the first decade of the new century. Or if they did, very few people could see the catastrophe that was coming, or the events in the Balkans that would ignite it. The country was about to be robbed of the very best from an entire generation. In those days, few people knew about Bosnia, Serbia and Croatia.

Everything was happiness and light on Tresco.

In St Mary's Roads, the mighty fleet lay at anchor, the symbol of British power that protected the trade routes of the merchants that brought back wealth to the Motherland.

Thomas Algernon was no doubt delighted to receive a visit from his younger brother Arthur – or to give him his full title Captain Arthur Smith Dorrien, RN. Arthur was the commanding officer of HMS *Rainbow*, a cruiser of the Home Fleet that occasionally put into Scilly during manoeuvres. Arthur is the one studiously not looking at the camera in the photo below. It was a great boost to the local economy to have the fleet in, and there was a whirl of social activity at all levels of island society.

Rainbow looked like a ship built for comfort not speed, but she was escorted by the very latest in exciting maritime design – the ships that every young

The cruiser HMS Minerva *in St Mary's Roads, 1902.*

The Channel Fleet anchored in St Mary's Roads.

Captain Arthur Smith Dorrien, commanding officer of HMS Rainbow, *is seated, second from the left.*

New Zealand rhea were introduced to the duckery in front of Tresco Abbey.

officer wanted to be in – the Devonport Destroyer Squadron. These were fast rakish vessels capable of very high speed and armed with torpedoes.

The larger ships, battle ships like *Revenge,* the old fashioned flagship *Alexandra* and of course *Rainbow* represented the old Navy both in terms of equipment and officers. It was a time of change, and soon, in 1905, the very latest weapon would be launched that would make all but the destroyers obsolete at a stroke – the *Dreadnought.* It would also once and for all remove any possibility of Scilly being needed as a naval base – the water simply wasn't deep enough for a Dreadnought.

In 1905 they opened a golf course on St Mary's, and on Tresco they introduced New Zealand rheas to the 'duckery' around the pool in front of the Abbey.

Picnics and sailing took place in an idyllic world, when Income Tax was still only 3d (1.5 pence) in the pound.

The Devonport Destroyer Squadron.

Arthur with his bride and family.

In 1909 Thomas Algernon's oldest son, Arthur Algernon, reached his 33rd birthday, and took a beautiful bride – Eleanor Bowlby. They returned from their honeymoon and entertained the islands to a splendid party on Tresco. It must have been the highlight of the decade for many – the sublime moment before the storm that was only five years away.

Landing the fish, New Grimsby.

This rope slide was an exciting simulation of flight and was popular with everyone – ladies included.

CHAPTER NINE

SHIPWRECK! – THE *THOMAS LAWSON*

The Edwardians were an imaginative and confident breed, excited by the speed of history and anxious to push the boundaries of technology. By the start of the 20th century oil had become a valuable commodity, and the need to export it in bulk was essential. Obviously this could only be done by ship and soon the first oil-tankers were being constructed.

It was also a time when sail was struggling to survive against steam power. The *Thomas W Lawson* project was a bold and imaginative attempt by the Coastwise Transportation Co of Boston, USA, to prove that gigantic steel sailing vessels with small crews were practical and economical alternatives to steam. It is a dream that is still alive among marine architects today.

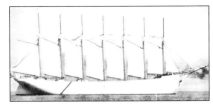

The Thomas W Lawson.

The seven-masted *Thomas W Lawson* was designed by Bowdoin B. Crowninshield and built in 1902 by the Fore River Ship & Engineering Company of Quincey, Massachusetts, USA for the sum of $258,000.

She was a magnificent sight – the largest fore-and-aft schooner that the world had ever seen: 5,128 tons, 376 feet long with a 50-foot beam. The seven masts were called Fore, Main, Mizzen, Number 4, Number 5, Number 6, and Spanker. However, the crew referred to them by the days of the week. She carried 25 sails in all, 7 gaffsails, 7 topsails, 6 staysails and 5 jibs. The total sail area of 43,000 sq feet was equivalent to an acre, and weighed 18 tons in all.

She was the only seven-master ever constructed and the largest sailing ship ever built. She had been originally designed to carry coal for the trans-Pacific trade, and was capable of loading over 9,000 tons, but later she was fitted out with internal tanks for oil. She was rebuilt in 1906 at the Newport News Shipbuilding & Drydock Co. for carrying oil in bulk. The topmasts were removed and the lower masts were used to vent the holds from oil gases.

Only when deeply loaded would she sail properly, but when full of cargo her draft exceeded that of almost all harbours where her cargo was needed. She was renowned as a poor sailer under almost all conditions.

A similar-sized steam-ship would have had a crew of up to 50 men, a fully rigged sailing ship of those days carried a crew of 28 – but thanks to mechanical aids for sail handling, notably steam-driven donkey engines, the *Thomas W Lawson* needed a crew of only 18.

She was an economical wind-driven cargo-carrier of impressive size, but handled like a beached whale.

The ship had been named after Thomas William Lawson (1857–1925) an extraordinary and flamboyant financier and oil company speculator from Boston, Massachusetts.

Lawson was also famous for his readable books and magazine articles about finance and the stock market. One of them was a novel called *Friday the Thirteenth* and was published in 1907. A curious co-incidence, as later events were to prove.

On 20 November 1907, under charter to the Anglo-American Oil Company and with a full cargo of 60,000 barrels of crude oil, the *Thomas W Lawson* slipped her moorings in Philadelphia harbour and set sail for London. The forecast was bad, and she ran into storms almost immediately.

Nineteen days later, on Monday 9 December, a hard southerly gale sprang up which lasted through Tuesday and Wednesday. The ship was raked by massive seas and everything on deck was smashed – including all the lifeboats. Most of her canvas was shredded or carried away – she had just six sails left – and many of her hatches were stove in.

UNLUCKY FRIDAY THE THIRTEENTH

On the afternoon of Friday 13 December – in filthy weather – they sighted land and what appeared to be another sailing ship. The 'ship' turned out to be the Bishop Rock lighthouse, but by the time they realised it, they were already inside the light and in big trouble.

They were trapped in the Western Rocks without room to wear or enough canvas to tack. Captain Geoffrey Dow recognised the extreme danger of his position and decided to drop anchor and wait. They were in Broad Sound, inside the Bishop and between Gunner and Nundeep Rocks. A severe north-westerly gale was blowing and the seas were mountainous.

The keepers of the Bishop Light immediately saw the peril in which the *Lawson* lay. The gale was increasing as the lighthouse men signalled St Agnes and raised the alarm.

The men of St Agnes launched their lifeboat at 4 pm and reached the *Lawson* an hour later. Incredibly, Captain Dow declined their offer of assistance. But they stood by anyway – making fast to her stern – and were later joined by the St Mary's lifeboat.

The St Agnes lifeboat.

Convinced that he had faced worse storms than this in America, Captain Dow decided to ride it out, although eventually he requested that a local pilot come aboard. 'I guess I'm alright where I am,' he said. Islander, Billy Cook Hicks, a Trinity House Pilot, boarded the *Lawson* from the St Agnes lifeboat.

The St Mary's lifeboat then broke her mast while manoeuvring under the counter of the *Lawson*. She returned to St Mary's for repairs and to telegraph for tugs to come out from Falmouth on the mainland.

It was then discovered that W F Hicks – one of the St Agnes lifeboat crew – had come out without oilskins and was suffering from extreme hypothermia. It was decided to return with him to St Agnes. Billy Cook Hicks stayed on board the *Lawson* with strict instructions to light a flare should further assistance be required. But no one informed the St Mary's lifeboat that the St Agnes boat had returned to her station on St Agnes.

The crew of the St Agnes lifeboat.

A KEEN LOOKOUT IS KEPT ON ST AGNES

They stayed up all night on St Agnes watching the pitching lights of the *Lawson* out in the Sound. At 2.30 am violent squalls and rainstorms cut visibility to a few hundred yards. When the squall cleared at 2.50 am, no lights were visible from the *Lawson*.

The men of the Slippen.

The crew of the Slippen *after looking for bodies.*

They desperately hoped that the lights had been temporarily extinguished by the squall, but at daybreak the terrible truth was apparent. All they could see was wreckage being tossed on the surface of the huge seas.

On St Agnes they were dumbstruck. A voice called for action. It was Freddie Cook Hicks, the son of the pilot they had left aboard the *Lawson*.

Eight men – five named Hicks – took the gig *Slippen* to search the rocks. They saw forms of men on the island of Annet, but on landing in huge seas at about 8 am they discovered them to be corpses lashed to wreckage. Then, on searching the island, they discovered the unconscious body of George Allen, a Battersea man, whom they managed to revive. He was suffering from exposure and broken ribs, and they rushed him back to St Agnes and a warm bed.

Later, two men were seen on Hellweathers Rocks. One was the Engineer – Edward Rowe of Boston – who was persuaded to tie a rope round himself and jump back into the sea to be pulled aboard the *Slippen*. His cries of agony were pitiful to hear. They took him to St Agnes before returning to save the other man – Captain Dow – who, Rowe had told them, was seriously injured.

Four men managed to get within yards of the injured man – but a gully separated them. It was young Freddie Cook Hicks who volunteered to swim to the injured man with a rope and bring him over.

The Captain, a very big man, almost helpless with injury and exposure, needed three men to help him back to the *Slippen*. He told them that at about 3 am huge waves swept many of the deck-hands into the sea. The squalls then snapped first one anchor cable, then the other. He ordered life jackets to be donned, and every man for himself. He took to the mizzen rigging with the pilot, engineer, mate and others, and had been in the sea for two hours before clambering onto the rock.

This was the account of Engineer, Edward Rowe, of Boston, Massachusetts:

> *"When the cables parted, the Captain, Pilot, Mate and I climbed into the mizzen rigging, each with a fathom of rope... When the ship struck I dropped onto the deck and the sea carried me overboard. I went under her quarter and passed right under her keel. I came up on the other side and found myself entangled in the rigging of the mast which had fallen overboard. I struggled for a very long*

time. I thought of giving up but at last by a supreme effort, I escaped and surfaced to find myself on top of a boiling sea.

"I clutched at a piece of wood and was carried some distance. I saw a man with a lifebelt on and I shouted to him but he took no notice. After a quarter of an hour, I saw the man again and induced him to come and hold the same piece of wood as myself. As we were washed along I felt another piece of wood rise between my legs and I wound my legs round it. I now felt certain of being saved, because it struck me that I was riding on a cross.

"The two of us were rushing straight at two large rocks with an opening between them. As we neared them, I released my hold on the cross piece and clung to the piece between my legs. I was lucky, the other man was not so lucky. I never saw him again."

'All that could be seen the next day was half the hull...'

The Slippen *crew are congratulated by Thomas Algernon Dorrien Smith.*

The *Lawson* had split between the sixth and seventh masts, and today the two halves lie quarter of a mile apart.

The US Government and the *Lawson's* owners awarded gold medals to the boat crews, and a gold watch to Freddie Cook Hicks. The *Slippen* crew were also invited up to the Abbey to be congratulated in person by Thomas Algernon.

Scilly became the first place in the world to suffer major oil pollution – ironically from a sailing-ship wreck.

The Inquest agreed that no lifeboat could have survived in the heavy seas after about midnight that night. George Allen died of his injuries – the body of pilot Billy Cook Hicks, father of brave Freddie, was never found.

CHAPTER TEN

island race   proud of it...

A Waffle with "The Commodore"

'The Commodore' is proud to be an Englishman.....

Scillonians suffered in the 1870s and 1880s as steam took over from sail, and many of their trades became redundant. Only Thomas Algernon Dorrien Smith's foresight in establishing the flower trade prevented a relapse into serious poverty.

Scillonians then were as hard as the granite islands on which they lived. Tempered by the elements, each man knew how to handle a boat, how to read the wind and tides, and each had an abiding respect for the sea – since there was hardly a family on Scilly that had not lost a member to Davy Jones at some time. This was a world where men were judged by what they did, not by what they said.

Look at the pictures on page 15 of the German fleet sheltering in St Mary's Roads from a storm during the Franco-Prussian War of 1871. All are sailing ships.

Yet 30 years later the 1901 photographs of a division of the Channel Fleet occupying the same anchorage show steam-powered cruisers and battleships. And what a fleet! A greater tonnage of ships was anchored in St Mary's Roads than exists in the entire Royal Navy of today. They were mightily impressive with glittering brightwork, spotless decks and vast white ensigns.

Battleships and cruisers of the Home Fleet in St Mary's Roads, 1901.

The battleship HMS Magnificent, *second flagship of the Channel Fleet.*

THE CHANNEL FLEET IN ST MARY'S ROADS, 1902

The battleship HMS Majestic, *first flagship of the Channel Fleet, later sunk in seven minutes by a torpedo in 1915.*

HMS Diadem

The flagship of the Channel Fleet.

The cruiser HMS Diadem, *armed with sixteen 6" guns.*

The cruiser HMS Niobe.

LAND OF HOPE AND GLORY

1902 was also the year when the country's second great anthem was played for the first time. It enraptured the Edwardians, summing up their confidence and belief in their national identity and the virtue of an Empire on which the sun never set.

HMS Dasher.

> *Land of Hope and Glory, Mother of the Free,*
> *How shall we extol thee who are born of thee?*
> *Wider still and wider shall thy bounds be set;*
> *God, who made thee mighty, make thee mightier yet.*

But the poet Rudyard Kipling had felt the cold shadow of future events five years earlier and penned his prophetic *Recessional* in 1875.

> *Far-called, our navies melt away;*
> *On dune and headland sinks the fire:*
> *Lo, all our pomp of yesterday is*
> *One with Nineveh and Tyre,*
> *Judge of the Nations, spare us yet,*
> *Lest we forget, lest we forget.*

The Channel Fleet, steamed up and ready to leave.

Those who live by the sea or on the sea are united by a comradeship and the need to survive the ocean's moods. In Britain, no one lives further than 80 miles from the sea, and over the centuries Britons learned the importance of the sea to an island race. Command of the seas ensures trade, and knowing this, Britain had built the largest commercial empire known to History

No enterprise of the scale of the Empire could operate without laws, justice, health and education. It had been true of the Roman Empire, and the British, themselves once occupied by Rome, had learned the lesson.

The Edwardian Englishman was the epitome of the British Empire; renowned for good manners, sang froid, tolerance, a love of irony and sense of fair play – all perceived characteristics of his Anglo Saxon background.

In fact, the real strength and secret of the Victorian British Empire was that no subjugated people who were fed, educated and given a justice system would rise up against their colonisers. Thus in 1890 for example, just 6,000 Britons successfully governed and administered over 300 million Indians.

'Farewell'.

This began what the historian Trevelyan described as 'the finest traditions of Anglo-Indian rule among soldiers and civil servants devoted not to personal gain but to government as a means of peace and welfare for millions.'

A small island race had found a way to govern peaceably a quarter of the world's land mass and population by making each subject a British citizen.

'Rule Britannia' contains the lines 'Britons never, never, shall be slaves'. The slave trade was made illegal in Britain in 1807, and by 1815 Britain had

The Fleet always offered naval hospitality on board.

persuaded the Powers of Europe to follow suit. Slavery was abolished under the Union Flag after the 1833 Abolition Act and Britain paid out a massive £20m to businesses around the Empire as compensation to ensure that slaves became free men.

Britannia's mighty navy – just one small part of which is glimpsed in these photographs – enjoyed total command of the seas, there was no power on earth that dared dispute her determination that the slave trade would end.

Despite appeals from West African chiefs who had lost a profitable business, the Royal Navy mounted a blockade of African ports to eliminate the trade once and for all. Hundreds of British sailors died of disease while enforcing this blockade. Then, the Union flag and White Ensign were specially associated with the freedom of the black man.

After the Second World War Britain's colonies had to fend for themselves as independent nations. Many, notably African, took a fast-track back towards the Stone Age. The Indian sub-continent on the other hand learned from the British, as Britons had learned from the Romans, and they prospered.

The Motherland opened the door to her overseas subjects, and Britain changed from a mono-culture to a multi-culture. The nation successfully absorbed many different creeds and colours of skin. Just as Celt, Saxon, Norman and Jew had been absorbed over the previous two millennia, so Hindu, Moslem, Buddhist have become part of, and enriched, British society.

They came from every corner of the world where Britain had her colonies, arriving from countries that twice in the 20th century had sent their sons to fight and die for King and Empire.

Today there are no hyphenated nationalities in Britain. No one describes themselves as Jewish-British, African-British, or Indian-British. Each is simply British; protected by the precedent of our Roman and Saxon ancestors in an unwritten constitution.

The Empire disbanded peaceably, quickly and humanely. Independence was granted to every country that craved it, although for some it proved rich for the blood. Today we have a Commonwealth, over which our Monarch presides – not with any power, but in the hope of continuing to pass on civilised values honed over two thousand years.

No battle-cruisers, gunboats or armies are there to enforce the values of the world's oldest democracy. In celebrating Britain's peaceful assimilation of the many cultures that enrich us today, it is easy to forget all those Britons who died in swamps, jungles, deserts and mountain passes to maintain Pax Britannica – a world peace that allowed many nations to develop, and one in particular across the Atlantic to emerge as a Superpower. The baton had been passed on.

CHAPTER ELEVEN
RNAS – TRESCO

FIRST WORLD WAR SEAPLANE BASE

Thomas Algernon was 68 when the Great War started. Scilly had been saved from becoming a naval dockyard in the 19th century, but now there was a new menace – German submarines. The islands were needed as a base for seaplanes that could spot the U-boats, and maybe destroy them. Tresco was the perfect place to build a Naval Air Station.

Tresco's involvement in the terrible Great War was brief but effective. Royal Naval Air Station Tresco was created in 1917 and reached its zenith in the final days of the War, by which time it was a fully functional seaplane base with a vital anti-submarine role.

By the end of the war it had changed its name when, in April 1918, the Royal Naval Air Service was merged with the Royal Flying Corps and the base became known as RAF Tresco.

At the start of the Great War in 1914, Belgium fell to the Imperial German Army and Ostend and Zeebrugge became bases for the German Navy.

Britain, as an island, had to import vast quantities of food and raw materials by sea to survive. Germany's strategy was to cut off Britain's supplies, and the most effective weapon to do it was the deadly U-boat, or submarine.

By 1915, the German navy had sunk several British warships in their home waters, including the battleship *Formidable* off the Dorset coast. Soon they were operating in the Atlantic and Irish Sea. In one day, 12 March, the German submarine U-29 sank four ships off Scilly.

The British response was to mount airship patrols to detect U-boats, and bases were constructed on mainland Cornwall. In 1916 work was completed on Tresco to allow airships to moor there between patrols, but the exposed nature of the site meant it was not used often. But airships were proving effective on both sides. British airships drove off several U-boat attacks on convoys, and German Zeppelins bombed London and Liverpool.

Airship C9 over Tresco.

In January 1917, it was decided to use float-planes against the U-boats and an experimental base was established at Porth Mellon on St Mary's. This proved too exposed, and operations were switched to the more sheltered New Grimsby harbour at Tresco.

At the same time, two destroyers arrived at Scilly to carry out trials on a man-carrying kite designed to be towed astern of a fast-steaming destroyer. The idea was to raise an observer to detect U-boats, or other vessels over the horizon. It was a concept developed by Samuel Franklin Cody from America. Various brave men volunteered to be lifted aloft but the concept never worked very well in practice. A proposal to drop men silently at night behind enemy lines in Flanders from a man-carrying kite was tested elsewhere but sadly was never successful.

....

57

SS Great City torpedoed and aground in Tresco Channel.

U-29 *about to sink SS Headlands off Scilly.*

Norwegian ship after being shelled by a U-boat off Scilly.

SS Gull Flight an American ship torpedoed off Scilly.

SS Eastgate torpedoed and aground.

Tents in New Grimsby.

Eventually in 1917 it was decided to put Royal Naval Air Station Tresco on a fully operational footing. Tents were erected in the field at the bottom of the Abbey drive next to the Great Pool and No 1 Air Construction Corps moved in. Permanent buildings, a metal hangar, canteen and a substantial slipway for the retrieval and launching of seaplanes were constructed – and for the first time motorised transport ran on the roads of Tresco. The vehicles were marked ACC for the Air Construction Corps.

A revolutionary floating refuelling dock for seaplanes was designed by one of the naval pilots – Edward Burling – who later achieved fame by becoming the first man ever to be catapulted in an aircraft from a ship. But this would not happen until 1924, in HMS *Vindictive*. A wireless station was also constructed on the island, high above New Grimsby.

Air Construction Corps transport on Tresco.

Mr A E Bull had been a school-teacher before he was conscripted into the Royal Naval Air Service. Later, in 1973, he wrote about his time helping to build RNAS Tresco in a letter to islander Roy Cooper. He also kept a photograph album, from which many of these pictures are taken.

'It was in the October of 1917 that I first came to know Tresco, and it was in many ways my good fortune to be stationed there for fifteen months. I had joined the Royal Naval Air Service and after two months at a training camp in Norfolk, I was one of a draft sent to Tresco; a Cornish man at the camp told me that that it was one the islands in the Isles of Scilly.

New Grimsby, 1917. The seaplane refuelling dock in the bay, invented by Edward Burling.

A painting by Edward Bull from 1917 when he served on Tresco.

Destroyer alongside in St Mary's, after hitting the Crim.

'We were to join a larger force called the Construction Corps. Work was already in progress at New Grimsby on permanent quarters for men of the RNAS small seaplane base.

'Our section camped in bell tents near the sea but this proved too exposed and the camp was moved. The new site was a rectangular site south of the Great Pool; it was more sheltered and better laid out. The entrance, still there, sloped down and at an angle to the road. The trees on each side are probably successors to the more robust ones that I remember. Those at the eastern end of the field seem the same as the ones I knew. I sometimes walked through them to the Gardens. The view of the lake was as it is now, and I well remember how the islanders prophesied that we should all have rheumatism; fortunately, they were wrong.

'Our four lines of bell-tents ran parallel with the road beginning level with the entrance and running east, with I think six or eight in a line, and four men sleeping in each tent. To the left of the entrance was a large marquee that served as a meals tent. On the lake side of this was a wooden recreation hut – there may have even been two.

'Technically, we were in the Navy and so had hammocks but since we could not 'sling' them we were entitled to sixpence a night 'hard lying' money which we duly received until later when we were merged with the RAF. Thin mattresses, blankets etc were part of our kit and many tents had wooden floors, so the lying was not specially hard!

'In the first December we were there a very fierce westerly wind struck the islands and almost flattened our camp. All through the night we strove to keep the guy-ropes tight, but some tent poles broke and by the morning most tents were flat – including the marquee. With the gale still blowing we were instructed to carry – a difficult job in the wind – camp equipment and our belongings to a large barn in New Grimsby which had a good upper floor, and this had to be our 'home' for a while.

'Two large flying-boats, built in mahogany marine plywood were anchored off Bryher in Cromwell Sound. There had not been time to get them onto the slipway, and the wind flung them about until they broke up completely. The engines sank and for weeks afterwards we could pick up bits of plywood on the island shores. A naval motor launch rode out the storm away from the coast and rocks.

'In due course the camp was re-conditioned and improved. The tents, arranged as before, had each a circle of ground around them and the walking space was sanded. The perimeter fencing was covered with vertical bunches of rushes – on the advice, I believe, of the very knowledgeable islanders who were expert in screening their daffodil fields. Above this, on tall uprights wire netting was stretched – surprising to us – for a further windbreak. Certainly the camp remained intact afterwards.

'It was from this camp that the working parties emerged each morning through the gateway to the road, turning right and passing between two banks of New Zealand flax on the way to the site which was being prepared or on which huts were being erected. The site I think must have been somewhere near where the present builder's yard is. It had to be levelled and one considerable hillock of sand required the use of tip-trucks and light 'railway lines' to be transported elsewhere to build up levels.

'The huts were built of concrete which was mixed on a 'banker-board' by hand – we did not have a mechanical mixer – and taken in wheel-barrows to a 'Winget' machine and put into a mould for the type of block required, and then rammed down. Pulling a lever let down the iron sides of the mould leaving the new block on an iron plate ready to be carried to storage space to harden. In hut construction rectangular blocks with slots at each end built up the uprights down the sides, while L-shaped ones, also with slots, formed the corners. Both types had holes for reinforcing rods or 'grouting' with concrete slabs 2½ ins thick cast in moulds were lowered into the slots, thus forming walls with spaces left for doors and windows.

'Concrete also being used for floors and paving, there was a great demand for cement. This in 2 cwt sacks was brought by small ships, usually herring drifters in Government service. These could only berth at New Grimsby Quay at high tide and had to be unloaded without delay to enable the vessel to leave again. The unfortunate company on duty at the time turned out for the job of unloading cement and other supplies whatever the time of day or night. There was a store, brick-built I think, at the shore end of the Quay near where the little shop is now, and we had some small lorries for transport. These and a small Ford car for other uses were the only motor vehicles on the island, and the position was much the same on St Mary's.

'From New Grimsby Quay or from Carn Near (without a jetty as there is now) we could, when off-duty, go in the 'liberty boat' to Hugh Town, much smaller and quieter that it is now. But time did not allow much exploration. It had to be remembered that we were not on holiday, and it was wartime – affecting civilians as well as those in the Services. I was never able to visit St Agnes, although I have since.

'Unless we were on duty much of evening time was free, and part of Sundays. Some of the men had, or could borrow, a boat for a trip to Bryher. Teas at cottages were sometimes possible, but food rationing was a restriction.

'Three friends and I bought an elderly but still serviceable boat in Hugh Town, but kept it on the Old Grimsby shore, and so had St Martin's for our visits, having with caution and advice learnt our way. Sometimes an evening's fishing would add Pollack or Mackerel (if we had been lucky) to our or someone else's service rations.

'Living almost entirely on Tresco it was fortunate if one could find interests of one's own making; the population, apart from service personnel, was small. I can only remember one general shop, and food was rationed. There was, of course, no cinema, and radio in the home was still some years away. But at least some of us made friendly contact with the people of Tresco. As a teacher myself, I sought out the headmistress of the small school to share interests. She invited four of us to the schoolhouse where she lived with her mother. I have forgotten her name.

'We were sometimes able to use her piano for a little not-very-expert music, but very welcome to camp dwellers. On rare occasions we had a church parade at

Huts in New Grimsby in 1917.

Flower picking on Tresco around the time of the Great War – Mr Kelloway and Mrs Vernon.

Distributing the flowers to the cottages for bunching. Mr Kelloway and Mr Goddard.

St Nicholas church, and the Vicar kindly agreed to my occasionally using the church organ for an hour or two – with the help of a boy living nearby to 'blow' for me. It was a very small pipe organ with some peculiar features but very welcome to me.

'Other help came from the bailiff, as I think he was called. From him I was offered the use of part of his office, out of working time, as a dark room. I had a little folding 'plate' camera – there were no military secrets there! – and I took a few pictures of the flower growing and such subjects as might be of interest later. Some photographic supplies and some good postcards could be bought at the Chemist in Hugh Town where the present one still stands. You may be amused to hear of another service we had from the bailiff. Somewhere on the farm he showed us a rectangular pig trough scrubbed very clean, and he offered it to us as a substitute for a bath – a welcome one for tent dwellers. I forget how hot water was obtained.

'From various people we learned much about the flower-growing and were able to watch one whole season through with much interest and pleasure.

'The undertaking seemed to involve most of the people – certainly on Tresco. I remember the picking in the bud stage, the distribution with horse and cart to the

An aerial view of New Grimsby from an RAF plane. The slip is still there. The concrete bases for many of the huts still remain.

The finished hangar in 1918.

cottages, the skilful grouping, and then the final packing into cardboard boxes in a long glass-house. They were then ready for transport to St Mary's Quay and the boat for Penzance – a predecessor of the Scillonian *(was it the* Lyonesse*?).*

'It must be remembered that what I saw was under wartime conditions and restrictions, and doubtless with young men in the Forces. The German submarines were sinking ships in the approaches to Britain; they probably treated the dangerous waters around Scilly with respect. Our small seaplane base was doubtless intended for reconnaissance, and there was a store of bombs – small ones for the seaplanes to carry – and I remember that the north end of Samson was used for target practice, sometimes with live bombs.

'There was not much level ground where ordinary planes could land but I remember that once, to our great interest, a very small airship came from the mainland and landed at Tresco. The elongated balloon had slung underneath it a small platform with safety 'walls' (metal network probably) and on this was space for the pilot and one other, plus the motor to drive the propeller.

'It must have been in the middle of 1918 that work on a fairly large hangar was begun. It was a framework of iron girders and the foundations for the main uprights were based upon large concrete cubes (about 5 feet) filling spaces dug in the ground (mostly sand). There must have been qualified people in the Construction Corps and workmen able to tackle the placing and bolting together of the girders. I know that one man who previously had been working with a horse and cart proved to be a surveyor who then became responsible for accurate structural measurements.

'Another project which was begun and never finished was for a railway line from the quay in New Grimsby to the buildings. Ordinary rails and wooden sleepers began arriving and had to be unloaded and stacked even after the end of the War. What happened to these, I wonder?

'I have so far made no reference to the fact that while these things were happening in these fairly remote islands, the war with its ghastly long lists of casualties was raging in France and elsewhere, and the outcome remained in doubt certainly for the first part of the year. With radio then no more than messages in Morse Code and with newspapers not readily available, we listened to news or rumour which reached us perhaps from those who had been on leave or more directly when, at long intervals, we ourselves went. After July news brought more hope, but not until October was there talk of an armistice.

'But at home another scourge became widespread through the country in a very serious epidemic of influenza causing a large number of deaths. In spite of the distance from the mainland the disease reached Scilly and numbers of men succumbed to it – in a few cases fatally. How it affected the islanders themselves I do not know.

'But by now victory seemed certain and on November 11th at 11 o'clock in the morning an Armistice was signed, and the news soon reached us. It was my first day out-of-doors after being in 'sick bay' with influenza and I saw slung between the two tall wireless masts the message in naval signal flags saying (I was told) "Peace with Victory".

'The work we were doing now seemed pointless though some supplies (including the rails) for the work continued to arrive, but by January demobilisation was beginning.

'On a wet morning in January 1919 I left Tresco from Carn Near to board a steamer at St Mary's to begin my journey home. It was not until April 1972 that I landed again, with much interest, at the same point. It was then my pleasure to act as guide to my family party.

'Tresco was much as, over the years, I remembered it, and the views in so many directions remain unchanged, though my memory has been refreshed. As always the light, colours, mist and brightness are continually changing and the moods vary from the scowl of storm clouds to the glory of sunset colours reflected on calm seas between the islands.

A E Bull
Tenby, Pembrokeshire
(formerly of Surrey)
1973

It had been early in 1917 when Squadron Commander Hope-Vere moved operations from Porth Mellon on St Mary's to New Grimsby on Tresco. RNAS Tresco started flying missions in February 1917 with 6 H-12 flying boats. Many of the station staff were still billeted on St Mary's, while others – like A E Bull – occupied tents, and eventually wooden huts on Tresco.

Drifters moored at St Mary's Quay.

VARIOUS SEAPLANES
AT TRESCO.

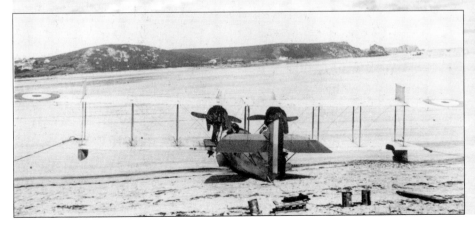

Aircraft taxiing in New Grimsby Channel.

Blast damage after the explosion.

The bomb damaged store being rebuilt. These are now holiday cottages Puffin, Tern and Kittiwake.

The rebuilt store.

In July 1917, Tresco suffered a serious setback when an ammunition store in the bothy (now holiday cottages Puffin, Tern and Kittiwake) next to New Grimsby beach exploded. Three men were killed and several injured. The men were on the beach, possibly arming bombs, when the explosion occurred.

Considerable damage was caused to buildings in the vicinity and also to equipment, but the site was cleared rapidly and by January 1918 the bothy had been completely rebuilt.

During 1917 aircraft from Tresco were patrolling an area that extended 85 miles south west of Scilly. They were also assisted by a fleet of drifters that did duty as patrol boats crewed by fishermen. By the beginning of 1918, two-thirds of British ships sunk were torpedoed within 10 miles of the coast. This was because the convoy system bunched ships together and left large sectors of the ocean empty. The frustrated German submarines were thus forced to take up operational station nearer the convoys' destination in order to have the chance of a target.

Aircraft from Tresco were soon in action against the U-boats. In May 1917 one of the H-12s attacked a German submarine on the surface that had been damaged in an earlier attack. The plane's two bombing runs were unsuccessful, all the bombs missing. The Germans proved to be tough prey, using their deck gun to fire at the aircraft and scoring a hit on the plane's starboard engine. The engineer climbed out on the wing to carry out a temporary repair to the leaking radiator, and they returned safely to Tresco.

Just three days later, however, a sister aircraft from Tresco sank a submarine with a direct hit forward of the conning tower. All the plane's crew received medals. This was the first success anywhere by a plane against a U-boat.

Damaged seaplane from Tresco, beached in Mount's Bay.

Tresco aircraft continued to carry out many missions against U-boats, as well as mine clearing. The latter task consisted of machine-gunning the floating mines from the air – simple and effective.

Mine-layers equipped with depth charges were also used against U-boats.

In August 1918 a Tresco seaplane spotted the White Star liner *Persic* crippled and under attack from a U-boat just west of Scilly. A fierce attack by the plane against the submarine drove her off, and the U-boat was later reported sunk. The crew of the aircraft radioed St Mary's for a tow for the liner that was then brought into St Mary's Roads.

Several aircraft from Tresco were lost in accidents, or destroyed in storms while moored off-shore, and three crew were killed when their attempted landing in a storm off Gugh resulted in the plane exploding.

A great many men and women were stationed on Tresco, and great efforts were made to keep them occupied whether at work or in their limited leisure hours. Sports days were organised in the summer and impromptu concerts and theatricals were staged. They seem to have mixed well with the locals, and there was no report of any friction in the community.

Many islanders themselves served in the War, 93 were listed on active service including coastguards and 19 lost their lives and are remembered in a Roll of Honour in the church.

Tired after a long life dedicated to the island he loved, Thomas Algernon saw out the War until his elder son, Arthur Algernon, returned unscathed. In 1918 Thomas Algernon died and the estate passed to his son Arthur Algernon.

A LOVELY LIFE... ALBERT STEEL, AGED 90 REMEMBERS.

I was born on Tresco in 1909, I am the youngest son of Frederick and Alice Louise. All my family worked for the Dorrien Smiths, my father was a top gardener in their employment. I had three brothers in the 1914–18 War. Fred the eldest won the Military Medal, Edward lost a leg, and Arthur the youngest was killed.

My grandmother was the Housekeeper to the Dorrien Smiths who thought very highly of her; they had surgeons come to Tresco to operate on her when she had cancer. She lived until she was 80 years old. Her tombstone is in the churchyard.

Ship's Company RNAS Tresco in front of the New Grimsby hangar.

A German mine lodged on the rocks on Bryher.

Testing depth charges from HMS Sprightly.

Sports Day on Tresco for RNAS personnel.

It was a lovely life on the island. We were poor but healthy. We made up for it by having our own boat and going fishing for pollack, mackerel and many other fish – including spearing plaice. When the tide was out we caught scallops, cockles and winkles. We had our own shrimping nets, it was a lovely life.

During the 1914–18 War we used to get up early in the morning to see what had washed ashore from wrecks blown up by the German U-boats. The story goes, I'm told it's true, the Germans never touched the islands because we buried some that had drowned. They are buried on St Mary's.

The five inhabited islands were St Mary's, St Martin's, St Agnes, Bryher and Tresco. Tresco being the best. My father was in charge of all the greenhouses, growing peaches, nectarines, grapes and other exotic plants. The climate was good for early flowers which were sent to the mainland for sale.

When I was a boy the islands were so thinly populated that we knew everyone on all five islands. We used to have gig races between the islands. All my brothers and sisters used to row in the boats, competing against boats from other islands.

Looking back to the 1914–18 War we had a seaplane base on Tresco some of the personnel used to lodge with us and take part in the Gig Races.

Unfortunately, there was an accident when a man on the base was doing something to a bomb when it exploded killing and injuring some. They turned the Working Men's Club and Reading Room into a hospital.

CHAPTER TWELVE
ARTHUR ALGERNON DORRIEN SMITH
1876–1955

Proprietor from 1918

Arthur Algernon – Major A A Dorrien Smith – was 42 with a distinguished army career behind him when he became the new Lord Proprietor.

From birth he had grown up among exotic plants on Tresco and he embraced the opportunities for travel that the Army offered. Apart from anything else it gave him a chance to collect plants from around the world while serving the King.

He served in South Africa between 1899 and 1902 and diligently sent back plants to his father on Tresco. In 1903 he was appointed ADC to the Governor General of Australia, and helped to set up the Botanic Garden in Melbourne.

Next, as a Captain, he joined a scientific expedition to the Auckland and Campbell Islands off the coast of New Zealand.

After getting married to Eleanor Bowlby he took his young bride to Western Australia, Perth and Albany. It was an uncomfortable and rugged trip, but one that they both enjoyed since Eleanor was herself a keen plantswoman. Together the newly-weds excitedly gathered strange and wonderful species to plant in the temperate climate of Tresco. Mostly, they were successful in transplanting their exotica in Scilly from the other hemisphere – exactly the opposite side of the globe.

They were inspired to write a paper about their honeymoon for the Royal Horticultural Society – 'A Botanising Expedition to Western Australia in the Spring'.

Plants were not the only exotica that he brought back from the Southern Hemisphere. Birds were hauled back to Tresco to join the 'duckery' – well stocked with rare ducks and swans, and also with rhea from New Zealand.

The First World War took Arthur Algernon away from Tresco, along with the 92 other Tresco men and women who served their country. His return in 1918 was not the joyful occasion it should have been – coinciding as it did with the death of his father.

In his absence during the war, the flower and potato industry had declined and was barely a profitable proposition anymore. Like so much else on the mainland, society had changed forever – the happy abandon of the Edwardian Age had been replaced with sombre reality. For Arthur Algernon – 'The Major' as he was known – it meant facing the fact that he could no longer afford to run the five inhabited islands of Scilly as his father had done before the war. Four years after inheriting the lease, he returned responsibility and control of all the islands – except for Tresco and the uninhabited islands – to the Duchy.

Arthur Algernon Dorrien Smith and his new wife Eleanor.

Arthur contemplates the future.

Miss Helen Dorrien Smith as a child.

This old hulk in New Grimsby harbour was always a popular picnic spot for children.

Storm damage of 1929.

He retained his position, however, as Chairman of the Isles of Scilly Council and held it for his lifetime.

Tresco Abbey Garden continued to go from strength to strength under the Major's guidance. There were sixteen gardeners employed to create and maintain not just the exotic plants but also the peaches, melons, and nectarines that were cultivated in the great glasshouses.

The Major was a plantsman of great repute and enthusiasm and introduced hundreds of the species that can be seen today. By 1935 the first list of plants of Tresco exceeded three thousand five hundred.

Summers were spent riding, boating, picnicking and attending events such as the island Fete, and the winter provided good shooting – including the traditional shoot on the uninhabited Eastern Isles in December.

Shooting on the Eastern Isles.

Between the wars, nature was not kind. In 1929 110 mile-an-hour winds ripped through the Garden devastating the plants and uprooting trees. The wind changed direction three times tearing into plants and knocking over 600 mature trees. It was a disaster, but with it came an unexpected bonus – new areas of the garden were now sunnier than before, and a programme of replanting established an even finer plant collection and a more open design.

In 1936 more storms and heavy rain caused severe flooding in Old Grimsby to a degree not seen since.

The First World War had advanced the aviation industry and, in the period immediately afterwards civilian aviation started to develop. It remained however a past-time of the rich. Learning to fly and then owning an aircraft was an expensive occupation. Neither was airline travel cheap. Passengers paid heavily to fly anywhere, and the days of cheap air travel for the masses was still half a century away.

The Scillies, and in particular the generously hospitable Dorrien Smiths, became an exciting destination for private aviators. After the unplanned landing of the *Columbia*, described later, various other planes made the trip either landing on Pentle Bay beach or in the case of seaplanes in St Mary's Roads.

Lord Trenchard arrives by RAF flying boat in 1928.

Flying boat passengers arrive at Carn Near on Tresco.

Some guests came to Tresco by flying boat in 1928 being rowed ashore at Carn Near. Lord Trenchard also arrived by RAF flying boat the same year to visit the Major. The Prince of Wales visited Scilly in 1933 to general acclaim.

In June1932, a Puss Moth landed successfully on St Mary's Golf Course.

Another visitor, Eugene de Veance, landed his Farman-Samson monoplane on Pentle beach in July 1935, after which islanders pulled it up to Valhalla, close to today's heliport, where it was parked ready for take-off. It was then hauled back to Pentle beach and refuelled.

In the middle of the Jazz Age, in the early thirties – a man that would change everyone's life, Adolph Hitler, was elected to power in Germany. By the end of the decade after his invasion of Poland, Britain was at war. With the Garden staff substantially reduced because of war service, the Major spent a great deal of his time personally tending the plants in between taking charge of the Home Guard. His wife Eleanor, with whom he had shared so many plant-collecting trips, took charge of the Garden, the island hospital and a small army of Land Girls.

Eugene de Veance's Farman-Samson, July 1935.

The Dorrien Smith family suffered terribly in this Second World War. Thirty-five men and women from Tresco served in the armed services, including six Dorrien Smiths. Four Tresco men were killed in action, including three out of four of the Major and Eleanor's sons – Robert, Lionel and Francis. In one terrible day Robert and Lionel were both killed in France in separate engagements. The family memorial in Tresco church remembers their sacrifice.

It must have been with great sadness but with hope for the future that Tresco gathered itself together after the Second World War. The Major and his wife threw themselves into the continued improvements to the Garden, introducing many unusual plants and planting more shelter-belts. By now, many of the exotic plants in the Garden had 'escaped' and seeded around the island, creating the island's unique sub-tropical vegetation that we enjoy today.

Refuelling in Pentle Bay.

In the early 1950s, the Major opened the Garden to the paying public and introduced a half-crown entrance fee. He also instituted an Agricultural Show on Tresco that did much to raise the spirits of the islands and bring the community back together again.

Towards the end of his life the Major received the Victoria Medal of Honour from the Royal Horticultural Society. He died, much loved and respected, in 1955.

THE FLIGHT OF THE *COLUMBIA*

Saying goodbye.

Errol Boyd thanks the RAF.

Refuelling Columbia.

On 9 October 1930 a small Bellanca Monoplane took off from Harbour Grace in Newfoundland, Canada. 23 hours later it landed at Pentle Bay 'near the small coastal town of Tresco' according to the pilot's log.

The 1920s and 30s were an exciting time for long distance aviation. In 1919 the first Atlantic crossing had been achieved by Alcock and Brown for Britain, in a Vickers Vimy bi-plane. In May 1927 Lindbergh crossed the Atlantic, and a few weeks later the feat was repeated by Americans Chamberlin and Levine in *Columbia*.

Later *Columbia* was sold to a Montreal pilot J Errol Boyd, a former Royal Canadian Air Force pilot, who took Lieutenant R P Connor of the United States Navy with him as navigator and set off from Montreal to fly the Atlantic on behalf of Canada. Bad weather forced them down on Prince Edward Island, and they then flew on to Harbour Grace to start their Atlantic flight. Although the name *Columbia* was still painted on the plane, Boyd had renamed her *Maple Leaf* and had the leaf painted on her fuselage.

They took off on 9 October 1930 at 16.30 and expected to land at Croydon Airport near London just over a day later. However, as they approached Scilly – after 23 hours – they started to experience problems with the fuel supply and decided to land. After a short search for a suitable landing site, Boyd decided on the sand of Pentle Bay and made a successful landing.

They found that a blocked fuel pipe had caused the trouble, and this was soon cleared. On Tresco they were put up at the Abbey by the Major, and the RAF from Mount Batten supplied them with aviation fuel. They were able to take off the following day for Croydon where a large crowd greeted them enthusiastically.

Columbia takes off, Pentle Bay.

CHAPTER THIRTEEN
SHIPWRECK! – THE *ISABO*

On 27 October 1927, the SS *Isabo* struck Scilly Rock on a foggy night at 5 pm. She promptly split in two just forward of the funnel.

On Bryher they heard a ship's siren that foggy afternoon bleating like a lost sheep. They knew that she was in serious danger. She sounded close and that meant she was already amongst the most dangerous rocks in the world, and there would almost certainly be only one conclusion...

So they opened the gig shed doors, and readied the gig *Czar* for sea. Seven oarsmen and a coxswain were the crew.

Norman Jenkins was in his 20s at the time, and half a century later he taped his memories for posterity:

'We went out in the Czar from Great Porth and when we got inside Scilly (Rock) we came on the wreckage with the men scattered through it amongst all this timber.

'The ship had broken in two as she struck... The timber was 27 feet by 8 by 5 inches and was used for keeping her cargo of grain from shifting. There must have been an acre – even an acre and a half – of this timber, tanks also, and casks.'

One of the gig crew that dreadful evening was a temporary resident – Baptist Minister the Rev. E R Pearce. He remembered:

'A terrible scene confronted us... huge iron tanks, broken boats, hatches, planks, spars etc. drifted on the surface, while scattered here and there among the ruins could be seen the head and shoulders of men clinging to the broken pieces of timber for support.

"The cries of the men in the water were pitiful to hear... they were so poorly clad that we had little to assist them by'.

Meanwhile, the Coastguard on Bryher had alerted the St Mary's lifeboat, although the instructions – 'at the back of Bryher' – were time-consumingly vague in the enveloping conditions.

The *Czar* doggedly continued in her task of saving lives in the fog, assisted by two motor boats from Bryher – the *Ivy* and *Sunbeam* – which arrived after making their way round from the other side of the island via Shipman's Head and through Hell Bay.

Norman Jenkins never forgot the scene:

'We took 14 men from the water, and the last one off the ship. When we had 11 on the Czar we didn't know how many more we would get, so we freed the gig for

more by putting them on board of the Ivy *and then went back and got four more aboard.*

'There were some men on the Isabo's *cross-tree. It wasn't possible to get to them or to the mate who had swum to Scilly Rock.*

'The worst of it was that some of them had nothing on but a vest or a shirt. You didn't know how to grip them. But we managed!

'There was one funny thing. We put one of them in the bottom of the gig and he put this bucket on his head. It seemed awfully funny to see him sitting there with a bucket on his head!'

Both the two motor boats, the *Ivy* and *Sunbeam*, started encountering real problems. The spilled grain clogged their circulating pipes and the engines became red-hot. So the *Sunbeam* then launched a small 8 ft dinghy which was responsible for bringing in 12 men. At one stage, a rope thrown to the wreck had five desperate seamen clinging to it. That night there was hardly a Bryher islander – or a Jenkins or a Pender – that was not afloat.

The St Mary's lifeboat – the *Elsie*, with Matt Lethbridge at the helm – was faced with a terrible dilemma when it eventually reached the scene.

Men were known to be in the fore-rigging of the *Isabo* but conditions had become appalling – darkness, heavy seas, floating wreckage – and then the lifeboat's propellers became fouled by a floating mattress.

The coxswain, reluctantly but with sound judgement, decided to wait until daylight.

Dr Addison was retired and suffered badly with rheumatoid arthritis. Nonetheless, he joined the island medical officer – Dr Ivers – aboard the lifeboat at first light. He recalled:

'When day broke, three men were seen clinging to the rigging, and one man in the crow's nest who seemed to be dead. The lifeboat was taken close to the wreck and three lines were fired over the foremast.

'The first broke, the second fell short, the third was successful but the ship-wrecked men seemed unable to make use of it, and successively fell or were washed off into the sea finally to be picked up by the lifeboat which made three trips amongst the broken water and rocks for that purpose.

'A man was then seen on Scilly Rock itself, a line was fired over him but he was washed off in trying to get hold of it so the lifeboat was taken in again and he was rescued.'

Two of the four men rescued were almost lifeless, but the doctors revived them as the lifeboat sped back to St Mary's. It then returned for a further – but fruitless – search.

Of the *Isabo's* crew of 38 who had set out from Lussinpiccolo in Italy, 28 men were rescued by the Bryher boats and 4 by the lifeboat. Of the six who were lost, one died in the rigging – but what exactly became of the others was never known.

One of the men rescued from the rigging by the lifeboat owed his life to Mrs Janey Slaughter who revived him with mouth-to-mouth resuscitation when he collapsed on St Mary's.

She then looked after him for three weeks. After spending that long awful night in the rigging, he was completely black-and-blue from exposure and bruising. Mrs Slaughter stated that when he was brought ashore she believed him to be an African.

Forty years later, Signor Rolli from Venice – by then in his sixties and a sea Captain – returned to thank Mrs Slaughter again for his life.

The memory of the night that the *Isabo* foundered stayed with Norman Jenkin's wife:

> *'I could hear from Bryher the men screaming in the water. When they were brought ashore we gave up our beds to them. We couldn't understand them and they couldn't understand us. But we managed to feed them. They were Italians mostly, but there were some Estonians.'*

The roll call of Bryher men – all who were heroes that night – makes interesting reading:

The *Czar* Crew
W E Jenkins, S Pender, W T Pender, F Jenkins, A T Jenkins, Rev. E R Pearce, N Jenkins and J J Jenkins.

The *Sunbeam* Crew
C Jenkins, E R Jenkins, S T Jenkins, J Jenkins, J E Pender and S G Jenkins.

The *Ivy* Crew
E Jenkins, S Jenkins and J S Jenkins.

Of seventeen crewmen, all but one were named Pender or Jenkins. Each was a father, son and a breadwinner to his family. Yet once again – as they always did – each selflessly put his life at risk to save others; strangers who had been wrecked on Scilly.

But there were also Italian heroes that night. The young 29-year-old captain of the *Isabo* – gave a graphic description:

> *'Within 10 minutes of striking the rocks in the fog she started to break up. The men and I ripped off the hatches and threw them into the sea to act as rafts.*
>
> *'I went to the bridge, but the heavy seas drove me onto the upper bridge, and eventually swept me off. Many of us were swimming or clinging to wreckage and were rescued by the Bryher men.'*

Two men who never made it were the engineers who stayed at their post in the bowels of the ship to try and keep power going, and then drowned as the ship broke up.

The 24-year-old mate was also swept into the sea:

> *'I floated on an oar until I got to a rock. I swam around to find the lowest place to land and came to a place where the sea left the rock 15 ft exposed.*
>
> *'I waited for a big sea to lift me over, then I struck in with it and came on top of the rock – still with my oar. As the sea went back I got a strong grip and crawled quickly up.*
>
> *'I was naked; I walked round to find shelter and eventually found a little cave, and I spent the night massaging my body for warmth and sometimes going round the rock to try and find other floating men. I found none, and did not know all night of the other men being rescued nearby in the fog.'*

The crew of the Isabo *pose with their rescuers.*

Before leaving Scilly, the men stood bared-headed on the Quay with arms extended in the Fascist salute, as their young Captain blessed their dead comrades left behind, and thanked the locals for their hospitality and heroism.

Count Leon, a local Italian resident, echoed these sentiments and urged the men to be as good during their lives as they had been during and since the tragedy.

The Italians then filed aboard the *Riduna* for the trip to the mainland, shaking the hands of the islanders who crowded round to bid them farewell, then giving them three rousing cheers.

An avalanche of letters, cash awards and expressions of gratitude descended on Scilly from the Italian Government, the ship's owners and friends and relatives of the rescued.

The Italian Government struck 38 silver and bronze medals and issued vellum scrolls of thanks – signed by the up-and-coming Marine Minister – Benito Mussolini. RNLI medals and vellum thanks went to the St Mary's lifeboat crew, Dr Ivers, the *Czar* crew, the *Sunbeam* crew and the *Ivy* crew.

The awards were distributed at a Town Hall ceremony by the Major – Arthur Algernon – who made an impassioned appeal for the resurrection of the traditional Scillonian gigs.

> *'I earnestly appeal that gig crews be organised and the gigs be put in repair. They may not be as fast as motor boats but they are more reliable and they still have a part to play in the saving of life.'*

The *Czar's* heroic efforts deeply affected the Church of England Minister Rev. Cyril Lancelot Thorrell-Barclay and he resolved on practical action. He appealed to the Regatta Committee on St Mary's for a special gig race.

To this day, the island men race their gigs every Friday night in the summer – including the *Czar*.

The Major's appeal was prescient. Twenty-eight years after the *Isabo* wreck, the gigs *Sussex* and *Czar* attended the wreck of the *Mando* in 1955 after she ran onto Golden Ball Ledge.

For one of the seamen rescued from the *Mando* by the St Mary's lifeboat it must have seemed all too familiar.

He had been the pantry boy on the *Isabo* in 1927, and was one of those saved from the rigging by the same lifeboat under the same coxswain – Matt Lethbridge. Matt's son was second coxswain at the time.

The wreck of the *Isabo* is just one of hundreds that dot the chart of Scilly. These wrecks live on in faded scrolls, in carefully preserved medals, in the memory of a few elderly islanders – and in the grand old gig the *Czar*.

It was a night when two Bryher families sent out all their menfolk to rescue unknown souls drowning on the Scilly Rock. It wasn't the first time, and it wouldn't be the last.

A haunting impression of that night came from the Baptist Minister Rev. Pearce who rowed in the *Czar* with the Jenkins and Penders:

> *'The experience of being so close to men in grave danger yet unable to rescue them is a terrible one.'*

For him, and for others on Scilly, the satisfaction of saving 32 sailors could never compensate for the sadness of losing 6 others to the sea.

The wreck of the *Isabo* was painted by the son of the Lifeboat coxswain, Matt Lethbridge, who later succeeded his father as coxswain of the St Mary's boat.

The wreck of the Isabo *on Scilly Rock, painted by Matt Lethbridge.*

CHAPTER FOURTEEN

SPECIAL FORCES IN WORLD WAR II

HEROES RETURN TO TRESCO

During the Second World War top-secret missions were made from Tresco that helped to change history. Boats disguised as French fishing trawlers crossed the Channel to ferry agents and documents in and out of Nazi-occupied Brittany. A modern historian has said that their achievements shortened the war and saved maybe half a million lives in the D-Day landings.

In 1998 I met some of the men who sailed in these 'Mystery Boats' – as the locals called them. What follows is mostly first-hand accounts of a secret war waged mostly by men barely out of their teens.

A more comprehensive account may be read in Sir Brooks Richard's book *Secret Flotillas*.

In 1998 Steve Ottery, the curator of the small museum on St Mary's invited me to a presentation at the Museum of a display board commemorating the Special Forces that had been based on Tresco in the Second World War. I am glad that I went.

A small group of maybe 30 men and women, all in their eighties, gathered in the Museum. Most were British, but there were also three well-dressed Frenchmen and an elderly French woman. In a brief ceremony, the display board outlining Special Forces operations of Tresco was unveiled and we then walked down the street to lunch at the Atlantic Hotel.

This is some of what I heard that day:

In the darkest days of the Second World War when Hitler occupied France, and Britain stood alone, a small team of young naval officers and men – French and British – carried out a series of top-secret operations from Tresco.

Their story has only recently been released under the 50-year secrecy rule, since for many years after the war the Government was concerned that the missions that they carried out from Tresco might one day need to be repeated should Europe ever be occupied again.

Listening to their gentle banter and quiet good humour one realised that in a world of so few real heroes that here were men of valour, dignity and chivalry. If Arthur and his knights really were buried on Scilly then they must have silently dipped their lances to those old warriors that day.

In 1942, as young and untested boys, they sailed from Tresco in adapted French fishing boats to Nazi-occupied Brittany. There they retrieved agents, dropped off supplies, and extracted the head of de Gaulle's biggest and best intelligence network in western and northern France. 'Remy' (Colonel Renault) and his family were snatched from under the noses of the SS –

together with top-secret German plans of all the coastal defences between Cherbourg and Honfleur. As a direct result of their achievement a great many lives were saved in the later D-Day invasion of France.

As they reminisced, one name kept cropping up. Daniel Lomenech. He had been their inspiration and leader; a Frenchman who had escaped from occupied France and who had an extensive knowledge of the Breton fishing industry. His widow and sons had come over from Brittany to be at the table with us.

The desire to see France free of the jack-boot burned deep within Lomenech. He had escaped to England from France at the third attempt in September 1940. By early November that year he had returned to France as an intelligence agent. After briefly returning to England before Christmas 1940, he left again for France with three others, but was compromised and came to England again for the third time, this time meeting a British submarine off the Brittany coast.

After this career as a secret agent in France he was assigned to a Royal Navy submarine in 1941 with the rank of Sub-Lieutenant RNVR. Their mission was to collect agents, passengers and mail delivered to the submarine off the Brittany coast by small French fishing boats. Lomenech was by then a mere 21 years-old.

It was Lomenech who suggested replacing the submarine with a diesel-engined trawler, operating from Tresco, which could blend in with the French fishing fleet. This would allow a more flexible schedule for the shore-based agents.

By early 1942, a 65-foot Breton trawler *Le Dinan* had been located in Newhaven where she had acted as a patrol boat. The Secret Intelligence Service (SIS) acquired her and refitted her. Sub-Lieutenant Steven Mackenzie took command with the young Daniel Lomenech as his First Lieutenant. The rest of the crew were mostly recruited from North Sea fishermen who were by then active service ratings in the navy – 'Jasper' Lawn, Cookie Nash, Jock the Engineer.

They sailed from Dartmouth to Tresco to put on their 'war paint' in New Grimsby. Every time they went on a mission the grey trawler that passed as a patrol boat in British waters would be painted in the colours of a French fishing boat. If anyone saw this transformation, the game would be up and the Germans might be alerted to the transfer of agents that was taking place right under their noses.

Daniel Lomenech photographed on Tresco.

The crew of Le Dinan *dressed as French fishermen.*

Le Dinan *in New Grimsby.*

Royal Navy officers and men at Tresco church parade.

Le Dinan photographed off Tresco.

So in the secluded sound of New Grimsby, hidden from prying eyes, they changed from warship grey and the White Ensign of the Royal Navy to a blue hull, brown upperworks, and a French name and number. In order to test the theory of passing as French trawlermen, they undertook two reconnaissance missions in May, on one occasion landing near Concarneau with impunity – right under the noses of the Germans. In June, after once again painting the trawler in New Grimsby Sound, they sailed on a mission of supreme national importance.

The *Confrerie de Notre Dame* was the largest and most productive of the Free French intelligence networks operating in Occupied France. The creator and head of the organisation was code-named 'Remy' (Colonel Gilbert Renault). The Gestapo were closing in on him – and his family. He had to be extracted from France with his family as a matter of supreme urgency. If any were captured and tortured the whole intelligence network might be compromised.

Some idea of the danger that Remy faced can be gauged from this telling paragraph from his memoirs.

'I had sachets prepared for me in place of the usual pills of cyanide of potassium, the taking of which causes, it appears, extreme agony just before death. Morphia on the contrary would give me – should I need to use it – a gentle sleep from which I would never awake.'

This is how Sub-Lieutenant Steven Mackenzie described his trip after leaving Tresco:

'We had an escort of Beaufighters to protect us half-way across the Channel, three planes circling widely about the ship, relieved in relays from St Eval. Even so, we had three hours of unescorted daylight sailing to put us 20 miles from Ushant by the time darkness fell. At 10 pm our air escort left us, flying low and waggling their wings in farewell.

"This was the most dangerous part of the voyage, crossing an area forbidden to fishing craft, and where a sighting by German air patrols would give the game away completely. We chugged on under a cloudless sky...

'By dawn we were south of Brest, the sea was like a mirror. At 10 in the morning we were among the crabbing fleet. As we sailed down the Baie-d'Audierne we could see the white villas shimmering in the sun. The lighthouse of Penmarc'h, the highest in the world, beckoned us on. Beyond it lay the Glenan Isles where our business called us.

'We reached our position with half an hour in hand. After an hour and a half nothing had appeared. Then at 6 o'clock in the evening black smoke appeared on the horizon, quickly followed by the appearance of five German corvettes. We held our course anxiously. Would they pass? Had Remy been caught and our plans uncovered? As the corvettes came on Jasper the coxswain nudged my arm and pointed to the islands. A tiny white sail had appeared. The excitement grew intense, the corvettes lent the final touch of colour to the situation. They passed us belching black smoke, the nearest less than a cable distant. We could see the captain examining us through glasses from the bridge, watched by German sailors on deck. We held our thumbs and turned our back on them. Then they were past, the casual inspection over.

'We watched the white sail tacking to and fro until the corvettes had disappeared. We let it approach until we could identify it; everything fitted with the description we held. 30 feet long, single mast, green hull... We made our signal, identified ourselves and went alongside.

'It seemed amazing that so many people could be concealed in that cockleshell of a boat. They had survived a German inspection when the vessel left harbour. Now they emerged. A woman first, then Mme Remy, then three children aged between 5 and 11, a man with several suitcases, and finally Remy himself – a parcel full of papers tied with string in one hand and a six-month baby in the other. They were helped on board, then the stores we had brought for the fishermen were handed over – petrol, oil, food and tobacco. In five minutes it was over, the warps were cast off.

'As she passed us to wave goodbye, the French skipper pointed to the sky. A patrolling Heinkel was approaching, but too far to have seen us together. We made gestures of contempt and then headed out to sea.

'We made an offing from the land and hove-to for the night. At dawn we began a slow cruise up the coast. Off the Ile-de-Seine an armed trawler came up from astern to pass close on the port side. As luck would have it, we were on top of a line of unattended nets; while she passed we stopped to haul them in, and were busy picking spider crabs from them when the officer of the watch swept us with his glasses from the bridge. A double triumph this, for Cookie had the crabs boiled in half an hour and we ate them on deck.

'The last and nastiest shock came at about ten in the evening. We were passing Brest, well to seaward, when we sighted three destroyers five miles to starboard. In a craft purporting to be an innocent French fisherman, we felt a little conspicuous as we made maximum speed northwards with dusk coming on.

'As though to confirm our worst fears, a destroyer broke away from the flotilla and headed towards us. For five minutes she held our course, gathering speed. We waited hopelessly for a challenge to blink from her lamp. Then she turned away and stopped. Exercise? We did not wait to see. The sky was growing darker every minute. We set about getting up the Lewis guns. From dawn onwards we would be in British waters, no longer in disguise, and allowed to hit back if necessary.

'At six the next morning, our air escort found us, and the children were allowed on deck for the first time. For 36 hours they and their mother had been shut up in the tiny wardroom cabin. They had not once complained.

Remy and his family were finally allowed up on deck once safely inside British waters.

'We did not make New Grimsby until three in the afternoon. The blue placid waters of the anchorage unfolded before us. White water boiled and tumbled on the rocks outside whilst within the water shimmered transparent and motionless. All was friendly, welcoming, unchanged. The place was deserted. But within half an hour we heard the drone of a Motor Gunboat's engines. Then around Shipman's Head she appeared, pennants fluttering green and white, bow-wave creaming the deep blue water, and from her loud-hailer came the martial crash of a Sousa march. She drew nearer, the music stopped, and we could see the cheery faces on the bridge.

'The passengers were quickly transferred to the MGB and N51 was left to herself in the anchorage to resume the drab grey of an auxiliary naval trawler. How many times she changed colours later, I would not like to guess. But the link had been forged: it endured for more than two years!'

Remy remembered the moment he arrived in safety in New Grimsby in his memoirs:

'We arrived at the Isles of Scilly. In a creek dominated by an old tower, our ship stopped, and tied up to a mooring. The water was wonderfully green and clear. The bottom which was at least eight metres under our hull, could be seen in the minutest detail. I could not resist the desire to dive in. I borrowed a pair of swimming trunks and jumped into the water which was as icy as it was beautiful.

'*While I was swimming, I could hear a fanfare coming from the other side of the trawler. The children were calling me to come back on board, quickly, quickly. I lost some time trying to find the rope ladder which hung down the hull and I missed the spectacle. Edith described it to me: a fast patrol boat of great beauty, long and white, shining in the sun, the crew standing to attention on the fore deck, all the flags flying, the sound of music (I learned later that it was a gramophone record played through a loud speaker) playing a military march, the officers on the bridge, standing to attention and saluting... a truly royal reception. I felt I was completely out of place, in swimming trunks and dripping with water, amongst all these uniforms, and I hid myself.*

'*The Patrol boat was an MGB (Motor Gun Boat) of large tonnage. We were made to go on board immediately and I dressed as fast as I could. We hardly had time to say our 'goodbyes' to the officers of our dear trawler: Mackenzie, Lomenech, Townsend, the delightful crew – and then we were off again.*"

Remy, clutching his parcel tied up with string, was in London within days. The parcel was soon in Churchill's hands. It contained a Nazi blueprint of the Atlantic Wall – accurate to the very last gun emplacement. A large part of the planning for D-Day was based around this document.

The plans had been stolen from the Gestapo by a professional house-painter and decorator from Normandy who went to SS headquarters in an attempt to get work. He deliberately quoted a ridiculously low price for the redecoration of the Caen headquarters of the German organisation whose responsibility it was to build the defences of the so-called Atlantic Wall. His offer was accepted.

While undertaking his work, the house-painter picked the plans off a desk and hid them behind a mirror in the room in which he was working – eventually removing them later. Incredibly, the Germans took some time before they missed the plans – assuming that one of their own number had taken them. They never solved the mystery of where they had gone, and the Todt organisation, whose office it was, was afraid to draw attention to the loss which reflected badly on their security.

Petty Officer Frank Rhodes served on MGB 318, and he described a trip that he made to Scilly

'*From our base in Dartmouth we were directed to Falmouth where we took aboard some 40-gallon drums of 87 Octane fuel which was to be transported to St Mary's on the Isles of Scilly. The Skipper and myself studied the maker's drawings to make sure that the drums were placed where there was adequate support below decks to prevent damage... and away we went.*

'*Without mishap we arrived at the Quay at St Mary's where we found that the fuel was destined for a Belgian Fishing Vessel which was fitted with deck tanks and bore an alternative Royal Navy number in addition to its Fishing Boat details – and either could be displayed. A Hall Scott engine had also been fitted. The crew spent ages transferring the fuel using a pump with two seats, one either side, and facing a pump handle whereby two operators could take turns to pump the fuel.*

'*Eventually, the fishing boat sailed and we were left to enjoy the relaxation of the Isles and the fresh dairy products, until some days later two RAF Beaufighters signalled that the fishing boat was returning. We went alongside to allow a passenger aboard, and he disappeared into the wardroom of 318.*

'*Immediately, we set sail for Falmouth and were cruising along nicely when Sparks reported severe interference on his radio. So I rigged the phones with long extension leads and shouted down the engine room hatch to isolate each bank of plugs in rotation (the routine for locating faulty plug leads).*

'Suddenly everything stopped and I was flung into the engine room to find smoke rising from the port engine. The starter contacts on the engine had welded together. The motor continued to rotate, finally seized, and took out the main fuse which supplied all power on board. Fire appliances appeared as if by magic, and the fire was soon out and the starter removed.

'The Skipper was rather concerned as we had the VIP on board, but he soon relaxed when we got away on starboard and centre engines, and then started the port engine by trailing in the port engine clutch. The whole incident took less time than it has taken me to describe, due to the superb fire-fighting training of Coastal Forces, and we made good time to Falmouth – and our passenger was placed on the train to London. I understand that he was picked up from a Fishing Boat in the Bay of Biscay.'

FRANK RHODES 2372

Another naval officer who spent his war in small boats with SIS was John Garnett. He wrote down many of his experiences:

'I joined the navy after one year at Cambridge as a volunteer in September 1941. I was sent to Collingwood to train and then to the battleship Malaya as a Topman. We were a heavy escort to aircraft carriers flying Spitfires to Malta. Based at Gibraltar I finally got off at Freetown on the 4th July 1942, and came home to go to King Alfred for a commission. At the end of my time I was asked to volunteer for special service. I didn't know quite how to get out of it, and knew I couldn't face my mother if I did, so I accepted and found myself at an office then called NID(C) later called DDODI (Deputy Director Operations Division Intelligence).

'I was sent to join a French fishing boat – the President Henot – then under overhaul at Shoreham. I was the First Lieutenant to the commander, Lt Richard Townsend. After overhauling our Deutz engine, converting the fish hold to a wardroom and a creating an enlarged area down aft for the crew, we motored and sailed in convoy down to Falmouth. We broke down on a number of occasions mostly due to filters and arrived in Falmouth in early December.

'At once we prepared for an operation to the Jument Buoy south of the Glenans, but after painting into French colours, between Tresco and Bryher, the operation was aborted due to bad weather. We returned after Christmas repainted again into French fishing boat colours and then set out from Tresco. We had on board wireless sets packed in tobacco sealed into French petrol drums. We carried little armament, just bren guns, and we flew French flags as required by the Gestapo for boats fishing out of Concarneau. There was a French name and French numbers on each side of our sail and on the bow.

'We arrived off the Jument buoy and on the first day failed to make the rendezvous with the fishing boat coming out from Concarneau. But on the second day there she was, and we transferred our cargo to her and took on board two or three French agents. At the time of the transfer we wore our naval caps, I remember.

'We had in our crew one Breton sailor Raymonde Leroux who came from Penmarch, on the north-west corner of the Bay of Biscay. He knew the fisherman in the rendezvous boat and there was tremendous dancing, and hugging and excitement at sea as they came alongside. We took on board a leading light of the French agents who brought over with him a rose tree planted in Lorraine earth for Madame de Gaulle, and a beautiful cigarette case bearing the Free French Cross of Lorraine, all made in France during the Occupation.

John Garnett as a rating.

John Garnett enjoying his breakfast during the mission.

MFV 2022 on a mission.

Lomenech at sea.

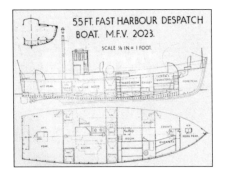

Daniel Lomenech and the crew of MFV 2023. Cookie Nash, Steven Mackenzie, Jasper Law, Daniel Lomenech and Joe Houghton.

'We then set out for home, and transferred the agents to a gunboat at Tresco, Having once again painted out all our French colours we put her back into grey and flying a White Ensign returned to Falmouth.

'The operation that I have described had been running for more than a year before I joined the In-Shore Flotilla. The leading light was Lt Daniel Lomenech who was a Frenchman, but carried a commission of Lt RN. He and Lt Richard Townsend had done a number of operations. Daniel was a man of enormous courage and the stories about him were legion. On one occasion when seeing a floating mine, he approached it and poked it with his boathook! He had carried out landings in the Glenans burying post boxes in the sand, and finally had the good fortune to command the new boat specially designed and built for the work – MFV 2023.

Back in Britain, yacht designer Laurent Giles started work in 1943 to design a high-speed hull with a French fishing-boat superstructure. This would be the ultimate boat for the job, capable of a high-speed dash from Tresco under cover of darkness. Her speed would put her among the Breton fishing fleet by first light. This top-secret vessel *MFV 2023* was built at Cowes by Groves and Gutteridge

Inevitably it was young Daniel Lomenech who was given command. Sub Lieutenant John Garnett, his second-in-command, continues...

'She was built at Groves and Gutteridge in Cowes and had the lines of a boat from Guilvanec. She was a 45 ft trawler but under water her draft was quite shallow, and in her fish hold she had two 500 hp Hall Scott engines.

'No longer was it necessary to go down to Scilly to change colour and then cross at 6 knots. She could go up into Frenchman's Creek in the Helford river and repaint there into her French colours. Then after dark she would motor slowly out until she clear of British Radar range before turning on her Hall Scotts and crossing at 23 knots. She could appear to be fishing on the banks off the Glenans by dawn next morning, She could do the rendezvous and then travel back again through the next night.

'Thus instead of it being a 4 or 5-day operation from Scilly it became a 36-hour operation from Helford. Of course she had the speed; had she been intercepted she could have done something with it. If the other boats had been intercepted or challenged there was no way that they could have survived.

Plans by Laurent Giles show a normal French fishing boat superstructure built on a high-speed hull.

'There were always good stories surrounding Daniel Lomenech. For example, he had to take her back to Cowes for an engine overhaul when he was just finishing with the flotilla before re-joining submarines. They had to go in convoy because they were supposedly a 6-knot fishing boat.

'As they came up through the gate off Yarmouth on the Isle of Wight everybody formed up, as was proper, in naval seniority. The Hunt class destroyer went first, then came Daniel Lomenech as a Lieutenant RN in his little fishing boat. Behind came all the merchant ships and finally an armed trawler. Coming up to Cowes the Hunt class destroyer increased its speed because they wanted to give leave that evening. She went up to 12 knots, and the little fishing boat behind him went up 12 knots also. So she increased to 16 knots and the fishing boat did the same.

'Finally the Hunt went up to 20 knots and the fishing boat followed. The senior officer of the convoy on board the Hunt signalled to Daniel "What is your maximum speed?" He flashed back "You would be surprised", put her up to 28 knots, ran round the Hunt's bow and shot into Cowes. He had totally compromised the secret boat and there was talk about whether or not he should be court-martialled, but I expect as usual he got away with it.'

The weather often prevented missions from taking place, and also added to the difficulties faced by the navigators. These individuals performed miracles in guiding the boats to the exact buoy or rock in Brittany that would be the rendezvous point. The Brittany coast is one of the most dangerous in the world – even in perfect conditions – but in wartime, with no lights, it was almost suicidal to attempt what they achieved. David Birkin – father of actress Jane and married to the woman whose voice gave us 'A Nightingale Sang in Berkeley Square' – was renowned for his ability to get any boat to any rendezvous in any weather. His efforts were even more remarkable since he suffered from chronic seasickness, and wore thick glasses to correct bad eyesight. Without his almost intuitive skill few of the missions would have been successful. He proved that navigation could be an art as much as a science.

The Navy had to fight the weather as well as the Germans, as John Garnett describes:

'Of course operations never went perfectly and there were many false starts. There were tremendous complications in getting messages back to Paris, down to agents in Concarneau, through HQ in London and the wireless communications centre at Bletchley – and finally down to us at Helford or to our scrambler telephone hidden in the heather at New Grimsby on Tresco.

'Having finally got a rendezvous time, then off we would go. The weather could be quite appalling, with force 8 or force 9 and on a couple of occasions we simply couldn't make it against the weather. Of course the fact was that with those wonderful sea boats, if the crew could survive then the boat certainly could – but it could be a real battle.

'On one occasion the weather had been quite dreadful. The rendezvous was made and we were coming back out around Penmarch in order to head back up to Scilly passing 30 miles off Ushant. As we finally weathered Penmarch we hit something under water. We didn't blow up but we lost a blade off the propeller and we didn't think we could run the engine. So we set our sails, but we weren't going to weather Ushant. We then tried the engine and there was a lot of vibration and leaking oil. Keeping her tighter than close-hauled we managed to edge up round Ushant but we couldn't go on heading for Scilly. We then paid off and ran away down to Dartmouth, and managed to get her in like that.

'On another occasion, coming back with agents from a successful operation, we thought all was going well but you always paid for it. At about 2300 we were *crossing the neck of Brest coming up to Ushant about 30 miles off shore. Suddenly, just before the change of watch, a huge searchlight picked us out. We were bathed in light and we thought 'My God, a destroyer has got us at last!' We didn't know what it was, as we didn't know then about Leigh Light Wellingtons who picked up German submarines on the surface with their radar and then dived and dropped their depth charges. On this occasion God was kind to us and the pilot must have looked first and seen that it was a fishing boat and not a submarine. He didn't drop depth charges around us. The coxswain on watch never really recovered from that appalling experience!*

Sir Brooks Richards served with SOE during the Second World War and his book, *Secret Flotillas*, documents the Special Forces operations from Tresco in which he took part, as well as other activities in Northern France, North Africa and Italy. It was Sir Brooks who had arranged the reunion and the presentation on St Mary's that I attended. I am grateful for his permission to reprint the accounts above and some of the photographs.

Another young RNVR Sub Lieutenant with Special Forces on Tresco was Paul O'Brien.

Angele Rouge *alongside New Grimsby Quay.*

'The enclosed photograph shows **Les Deux Anges** *alongside N51, which had sailed from Tresco, in November 1942. We were offloading an agent – and a great deal of mail – with even more heavy stuff coming aboard for England*

'The other photograph shows the crew of **Angele Rouge** *– our secret high-speed launch designed by Laurent Giles to look like a French fishing boat. Both this photo and one of myself were snapped by JJ just before we set off on an operation in mid-September. Note the dummy wooden 'gallows'.*

'I mention the 'gallows' because it was on this trip that we were nearly rumbled. We were on our way home with two agents, and were off the Raz du Seine on a day of intense heat and unimaginable glassy calm when every sound seemed to carry for miles. We were meandering along at a couple of knots, purportedly fishing, but our net and trawl doors were just two buckets slung from said 'gallows'.

The crew of the Angele Rouge.

'To the agents' disgust, and ours, a convoy of two submarines and several escorting heavy patrol boats – rather like scaled-down destroyers – appeared dead ahead and steamed quite meaningfully towards us.

'As we were trawling, to have altered course more than a little would have been a give-away to an alert observer, so we had to grin and bear it as they closed on us and passed no more than 200 yards off our starboard beam. A few minutes before this, there was a goose-pimply moment which pricked the euphoria of the agents we had just recovered. A flight of Junkers-88s swooped over us and released some shiny objects! Recognition signals for the subs, I hoped. So they proved, but the agents thought otherwise and dived under the nets secured along the gunwales. JJ advised them to stay there!

'As the ships passed, they were so close that we could see the faces of the crew, leaning over the rails, listening to some lugubrious German love-song. I was observing all this from the forrard hatch, partly hidden by the coaming. Good, I thought, they can't leave the convoy to ask us for some fish – always a big worry because **Angele Rouge's** *buckets were a dead loss. This time, though, we had bought a deckload of fish from Newlyn, stowed in ice.*

'Just then, JJ in the wheelhouse suddenly put **Angele Rouge** *hard astern. There were literally clouds of smoke from the Hall-Scott's carefully hidden exhausts – not to mention churned-up white water and spray! Surely, I thought, this is curtains. They can't ignore that – but they did. They must have had a good*

lunch. It turned out that JJ had spotted, just in time, a large Seine net only 50 yards ahead – and he had to keep our twin props clear of that, or else!

'Ever so slowly, it seemed, the convoy drew away and a few hours later in the fading light we were on our way at a rate of knots.

'The agents were still aggrieved. They had expected us to run for it – which would have been fatal. But JJ had done the right thing, and we were there to prove it. When some years later he gave me the photo no wonder he had written on the back 'Wot, no fish?''

Back in the Helford river, John Garnett was in continuous practice with the specially made surf-boats. These were necessary for landing and retrieving people and stores in the rough waves off the Brittany beaches. He soon became an expert.

Meanwhile, a magnificent private yacht had been requisitioned to serve as headquarters for the Special Forces in the Helford river.

'One of the great moments was the coming of Lord Runciman's yacht Sunbeam 2, a three-masted schooner (which was used as the In-Shore Flotilla's headquarters). Later she dragged her moorings, her buoys bumping all the time under her stern. Lt Commander Nigel Warrington Smyth swung her around on the tide and took her down river, whilst they moved the buoys further out and then we came back up again and moored up fore and aft.

'At the time I was under great pressure from my new wife not to spend the evening doing that but to come ashore. However I thought it was my duty to play my part in this operation with Nigel. As it turned out later he had, sitting on his desk on board Sunbeam, a recommendation for me to have accelerated promotion to Lieutenant. He had decided that if I stayed on board he would sign it and if I didn't he wouldn't. So although my wife Barbara was simply furious, later on she quite liked the second shining RNVR stripe.

'I've talked about heavy weather, but of course there was also the problem of thick weather. On one occasion we left the Bishop light going south for the rendezvous and went way out as always around Ushant then made our landfall on the great light house at Eckmul on Penmarch at the top of the Bay of Biscay before turning in under Brittany and coming in on the Jument buoy, Richard Townsend was in command. It was terribly thick and we could not see the lighthouse. Visibility must have been down to a quarter of a mile at the most.

'As we came in we could hear the lighthouse booming and we could hear water breaking on rocks, we continued to creep in when suddenly out of the fog in front of us came a great seamark. We immediately turned about to steam out and ran straight into a German convoy that was coming round Penmarch with a German naval escort. To Richard's eternal credit instead of turning back into the rocks and away from the convoy, as no French fishing boat would have done, he came straight out through the middle of the convoy holding his course and speed. We kept Raymond Laroux on deck, and I was on deck as well. As we pretended to be washing down we were watched from the bridge of the German destroyer. The Captain's binoculars stared at us, watching us... we just kept on with our affairs and went through the convoy and out into the fog again.

'There were two parts of the intelligence organisation working on the Continent. One was the secret service SIS – MI6 – that dealt with intelligence and in the end belonged to the Foreign Office, and was represented by Anthony Eden at the Cabinet table. The other was sabotage – SOE – that belonged to the Ministry of Economic Warfare and was represented by Hugh Dalton. These two organisations were utterly split from top to bottom, right down to even the most local level.

'In order to patch things up in the Helford River, they cleverly put Nigel Warrington-Smyth, who grew up as a boy on the river, in charge of SIS and based him on board **Sunbeam II**. Ashore was SOE under Lt Commander Bevil Warrington-Smyth, his elder brother. Finally, in order to make certain that the brothers always got on they put in charge of the whole Helford base Lt Warrington-Smyth, the Local Naval Officer (LNO), who was their father.

'On the whole although many plans were made, in the years that I was there SOE did nothing very much as far as I could discover other than practice and prepare boats. They were thoroughly cooperative and helpful but didn't do much out on the river. They had, however, an extraordinarily jolly young man called John Wilkinson, fair-haired and the son of the man who was the managing director of the Power Boat Company before the war. He was in charge of HSL (high speed launch) 115 that had belonged to the RAF and had been used for air sea rescue and could do 47 knots.

'John Wilkinson like many of the rest of us loved a WREN called Elaine Pilgrim. Her parents ran the Nansidwell Hotel, but as far as we knew nobody had ever made much headway with Elaine. She used to come to dances wearing a blue skirt with rings round it, and John Wilkinson was determined to have a close relationship with Elaine. So he let it be known to her that he was about to go on a most secret and difficult operation from which he might never come back. In the previous week he told her that he was to go on Tuesday night and that it was very stressful and worrying – and he was saddened that their relationship might come to an end because he would be lost.

'Finally on the Monday night when saying goodbye to her, he said that he expected to be back by 11 pm the next night and if he was not back by 1 am things were very bad and if not back by 2 am then it was all over. The following night, he never went to sea at all. He didn't ring her at 11 pm, 1 am or at 2 am, but waited until 2.30 am before ringing her up and saying that he was back safely. At which of course she tumbled into his arms.

'Whether this story is true or not I have no idea, but we all heard about it and thought that John Wilkinson was a bit of a lad. Elaine Pilgrim remained a simply lovely lady.

'This story concerns Christmas 1943. The work of running agents by boat to Brittany was partly done by fishing boats out of the Helford River, but was also done by two gunboats based on Dartmouth under the command of Commander Davies. Occasionally they borrowed other MGBs and crews from coastal forces. In November 1943 a gunboat had gone across to the north-west edge of Brittany and had landed two surf boats – 14' long with beautifully made overhanging bows to ride the surf. The weather was so bad that they were unable to get back to the gunboat. So the boats were taken ashore again, filled with stones and weren't discovered by the Germans. The crews were taken care of by our French agents over there.

'In the right moon period in December in the week before Christmas another gunboat went over to try to pick up the original crew together with all the people who had been there the previous month plus new people that had arrived to be taken off. The weather was so bad that the operation again failed. The boats' crews were totally exhausted, and there was nobody to man them for another immediate operation.

'On Christmas Eve, at dinner on board **Sunbeam**, I was called out to see Nigel Warrington-Smyth, the commanding officer, who said that we were to provide the boat's crews for an operation on the following night: the night of Christmas Day. In order to do that, because the numbers waiting were now so great – there were more than 30 on the beach – we would tow across the large SN6 – a 25' surf boat. I was to be responsible for the tow and for getting the boat there behind the gunboat as I was very keen on that kind of operation.

'The following day on Christmas morning I went in to Falmouth to get the charts and at 3 pm we towed down river with the surf boat behind the SOE seaplane tender 360, and out to meet the gun boat MGB 313 that had come round from Falmouth. We made her fast with a grass rope, with plenty of stretch and a wire as well and I sat aft on the gunboat all the way to France and towed her surfing on the stern wave of the gunboat. If of course she had got too far astern she would have swamped immediately, but if she could surf on the top of that wave then we could tow her at 26 knots all the way to France – 90 miles from the Lizard.

'Navigation was an amazing operation by the gunboat's crew. We were going into L'Aberwrach which is hard enough to get into through the rocks in peacetime with lights; and we were attempting it without any lights at all. The gunboat used an RAF direction-finding system where radio beacons gave a cross reference. The navigating officer brought us right up on the buoy, unlit, at the entrance to the channel. We then threaded our way up the estuary; on silenced engines, anchored, and a boat's crew with Howard RendIe as coxswain and 6 SOE oarsmen went ashore to Ile-Tariec which lay 800 yards from the gunboat anchorage. They had to make two journeys and brought off 32 people.

'Very quietly we turned and left for home. However, no sooner had we got 20 miles off than the gunboat's engine broke down and there was a good deal of worrying about whether the engines would get started again before dawn, but they did, and home we came.

'As was usual, the agents coming out of France gave the naval officers scent that had come out from Paris three days before, when I got back to Helford I went ashore at 8 in the morning and, it being Christmas, my wife was living in a house on shore. I woke her up and was able to give her, as a Boxing Day morning present: a bottle of Channel. When her sister saw this bottle of Channel on her dressing table, a week later, she said to her "Now I know what John's doing in the navy".

'Amongst the people we brought off there was an extraordinary faceless kind of man who might be anybody, and therefore you can't remember him. He brought ashore a roll of maps under his arm on which were plotted all the flying bomb sites right back to Holland. He had come across France, picking them up as he went and we brought him off in the extreme west. We also had a number of airmen on board. We had one in particular who had been flying in a Liberator which he thought was over Plymouth when he was suddenly shot out of the sky. He parachuted to the ground, ran to a road, stopped the first car and said "I am trying to get to Plymouth". The person replied "You're in France, you are near Brest, but you are in luck – get in". He took him back into Brest for the day and that evening, since he was an agent, brought him to be met by the gunboat. When he finally got back to London the next day he arrived only a day after he would have arrived had he landed north of Plymouth, instead of landing north of Brest.

'Among the 32 people we took off there were also a number of American airmen. They had crashed over France, and as always gathered in Paris where people were hidden much better that out in the countryside. They had somehow to be got back to England. They decided that since none of them spoke French the only way to handle this was to produce forged papers for the evacuation of a Deaf and Dumb Institution to the north west of France.

'False papers were made and they left the Paris station and came down to Brittany, They were unable to speak, and because of the shooting up and bombing of trains by the British, there were terrible delays and hold-ups and they went from village station to village station. The train got fuller and fuller. They were sitting on the floor and at one stage a woman got in with a pig in her arms and she let the pig slip and it fell onto an American airman's head and he immediately retorted "For God's sake woman take that damn pig off my head".

'There was a terrible silence, as they were meant to be deaf and dumb and clearly here was an American right amongst them. Nobody said anything, nobody tipped anybody off, and they came on through to a little station just outside Brest where they were brought across to join the MGB.

'This story is concerned with the time of the invasion. D-Day was on Tuesday 6th of June and of course we saw the loading from the river; we had seen the roads widened leading to Trebah beach on the Helford River in order to cope with the transport to American tank landing ships. We just lay in the river waiting for orders.

'On the Thursday, D+2, we were told to leave at once for Portsmouth in one of the fishing boats, MFV 2028, L'Oeure. I was to be the First Lieutenant on this occasion. We went up by convoy, got there during Friday and waited for orders. The orders were to join the convoy, on Friday evening, for the beachhead JUNO at Courseulles. That night we carried out members of SIS, the people we worked for, to reconnoitre the ground in order to be ready to pass agents backwards and forwards through the beachhead and the front line. We were to be the forward base. We anchored off Seal-View, Isle of Wight – my own home – and I was able to look ashore to where I had spent every holiday of my life, where my Grandmother was living, and my parents had built a house.

'We set out that night for area Z, known as Piccadilly Circus, where all the ships came in from all the ports of the south coast. There was tremendous activity in the centre of this vast area – south of St Catherines and 10 miles across. The ships went out on the swept lanes to whichever part of the Beach Head they were going. We were on our way to Juno at Courseuiles to get behind the "Gooseberry", the sunk ships which protected the beach. We arrived there on the Saturday morning and unloaded our ZEEP – the water-going Jeep – and contact was made by the headquarters people with the Commodore ashore.

'Of all the extraordinary things... on the Sunday, D+5, we were invited to lunch at the Lion D'or, the lovely hotel in Bayeaux. There we were sitting with French agents having lunch and paying in Francs printed in London. The previous Sunday they were trading with Nazi German Officers paying, no doubt, in Francs printed in Berlin. When later we went back to the Lion D'or, many years after, we discovered it wasn't a matter of just a week's difference. The front line had gone through Bayeaux on the Wednesday. They were feeding German officers on the Tuesday, and feeding British Officers on the Thursday. So in fact the French missed only one day's trading!

'After five days on the Beach Head we returned to Portsmouth to take another fishing boat back to lie over there to act as the reception area, for agents coming by MGB. We landed them and took them ashore, and we continued for two months with a boat over there taking it in turns. I was there for the vast bombing of Caen, with the whole sky filled with 4-engined bombers.

'I was also there for the terrible gales on D+12, when the worst northerly gales that had ever struck in recorded history blew down on us. We really wondered whether or not God was on our side. We in the fishing boat played a great part bailing ships out and helping with tremendous enthusiasm whenever seamanship was needed.

'There was a great moment when we were on the beach and things were very bad indeed – no ammunition had come ashore for at least two days. At that moment, who should come along the beach but a small man with a beret with two staff officers round him – and there was General Montgomery himself.

'What that did for the morale of people on that beach was simply staggering. Up to then, as a sailor, I had always thought that Montgomery was a bit of a bull-shitter. But there he was down there with us and we knew from then onwards it was going to be alright. He wasn't back somewhere, he was right up where the front line was.

'As the line advanced we moved our base forward. We spent some time on the English side at Shoreham and we also got a house in Dieppe. We then moved again with a base at Folkestone, running MGBs across to a house we had in Boulogne. At that point the operations involving the crews of the fishing boats from Helford came to an end, except for one crew of which I was the commanding officer. I was helped by a lovely New Zealander called Sub Lt Norman Ettlinger,

'We were told to man a beautiful Danish-type fishing vessel that had been built specifically for landing agents and sabotage materials on the Danish coast. Our job was to lie alongside at Dover and then to go over to Ostend and on to Rotterdam to carry stores for the agents in Belgium and Holland to reward them for what they had done for the Allies. In fact what they wanted was not money, which was relatively useless during inflation times, nor cigarettes, but bicycle tyres. So once every fortnight we sailed with our decks filled with bicycle tyres from Dover. This was an exceedingly happy time – based at Dover, then the coast near Ostend and then on to Rotterdam where we made fast to the tram-lines because the whole of the edge of the docks had been blasted to pieces.

'It was when we were back in Dover at 8 o'clock in the morning in the little ward-room that I heard on the news that the war in Europe was over – VE day. I can remember bursting into floods of tears of relief and being quite unable to stop myself.

'That night my wife Barbara was down in Dover as it was a school holiday, and we went to Canterbury to spend the evening of VE Day, and for the first time for six years the Cathedral was floodlit. This was an amazing end to the operations.

'In due course I went back to Helford to take Sirene round to HayIe for decommissioning and then later took 2032 back to the top of the HambIe to pay her off.

The epilogue
I went back to Cambridge to finish my degree; and then joined ICI as a clerk in Glasgow and worked my way up. In 1960 Barbara and I went for a week's holiday to Brittany in order to try to find SIRENE. We searched Domannes and various other fishing ports and finally on our last day in Brittany we came to Cameret. I walked up on the sea wall side, and Barbara was walking on the beach, At the same moment we came round and there Sirene was; lying on her side.

We heard that she was to be destroyed that Christmas and burnt because she was no longer of any use. We discovered the woman who owned her and went to meet her in a Café. She spoke mostly in Breton; we spoke in rather stumbling French. She told us how Sirene had gone out fishing and then disappeared and gone off to the 'gueru'. She had been returned to them after the war but she had been altered about a lot. I asked if I could take off Sirene some of the carvings that the sailors had done.

'There was a lovely little crest and a lot of iron work which was all going to be wasted and she said that I could. I went off to buy a hacksaw. We spent the afternoon cutting her main blocks off, together with a whole lot of her iron work and the little crests. We put these in the back of our Thames van and in due course came out through customs at Dover.

'I was very keen on listing everything I possessed for the customs. When the Officer read all this stuff, he said he didn't understand what all this was, could I show it him? I opened up the back door of the van. There was all this ironwork and he turned to me and said "There's no duty on junk." I said "It may be junk to you – it was our life's blood to us."

'The crest is in our boathouse in The Isle of Wight and the iron-work has all been concreted into mooring stones and so the dinghies lie with their chains fixed to Sirene's metal work. Her main sheet blocks are still used when there is a massive pulling operation to be done using a lot of children and grandchildren. In between times they hold the boathouse doors open.

'In 1992 at half-term, we took the young girls of my second family, with my wife Julia to Bayeaux and on the Friday we saw the tapestry of how the Normans invaded this country.

'The following day we went down onto Juno beach at Courseuiles, and saw where I had come ashore from 2028 as part of those who had brought freedom to Europe to get rid of the ghastly Nazis, their cruelty to the Jews and all Europe. We stayed at the Lion D'or, and there were many reminiscences, by them, and by me of 1944.

'On that second evening we went to a cemetery to show the 10-year-old and the 7-year old something of what it was about. There we read on one of the stones:

"Gaily he came, gallantly he left me, but I have his son,
a small sweet part of him".

'Charity the 10-year-old wrote in the cemetery book. "We must never let this happen again, we must make a better world."

'Since then I have been re-inspired by the thought that he died to produce a better world. We are lucky enough to have lived to make a better world. That is what we must continue to do.....'

I left the Atlantic Hotel late in the afternoon, and walked with Sir Brooks Richards to the Quay on St Mary's where we would catch a boat back to Tresco. He asked me whether it would be possible to erect a small plaque on Tresco commemorating the exploits of the Special Forces in World War II. Robert readily agreed.

So it was that a year later a small and distinguished party of 30 or so gathered once again on Scilly to unveil the plaque that was placed on a rock overlooking New Grimsby Harbour. This was the anchorage where the *Angele Rouge* and other boats lay before painting themselves as French trawlers and setting off under cover of darkness for Nazi-occupied France.

The unveiling party included General Sir Michael Rose, former Head of the SAS, and the Director of the Imperial War Museum. We stood with the few old warriors that were left. Daniel Lomenech's son, watched by his mother, pulled away the Tricolor from the plaque. Just below us, Paul O'Brien – a survivor of many of those Special Forces missions – stood in a rowing boat and addressed us. This is what he said in that early evening of 2 July 2000 as we stood by the plaque overlooking New Grimsby harbour:

This anchorage of New Grimsby Sound

N51 Le Dinan

Daniel Lomenech

served as a base for a secret naval flotilla from April 1942 to October 1943. British vessels, disguised as French fishing boats, penetrated deep into enemy waters off the Brittany coast to contact the '**Confrèrie-Nôtre-Dame**,' the most productive of the intelligence networks in German-occupied France.

In this secluded channel, the vessels exchanged their grey naval paintwork for the characteristic brilliant colours of South Breton fishing boats, taking care to avoid a freshly-painted appearance.

This sea-line of communications was devised by **Daniel Lomenech**, a 21-year-old Breton intelligence agent with excellent knowledge of the south Breton fishing industry. In June 1942 **Colonel Rénault**, head of the Confrèrie and his family, who were in extreme danger, were rescued in the vessel N51 'Le Dinan'. This expedition, commanded by **Lt. Steven MacKenzie RNVR** with **S/Lts. Richard Townsend RNVR** and **Daniel Lomenech RNVR**, also brought back a detailed plan of the coastal defences that the Germans were constructing along the Normandy coast. This information became the basis of the **D-Day Landings** of 1944 and ensured minimal loss of men and materials in that operation.

Holdsworth Special Forces Trust   2 July 2000

The plaque at Braiden Rock, past the quay shop overlooking New Grimsby harbour.

'Dear Friends and Scillonians

'This is a great day – and a memorable moment – for the families of the officers and crews of N51, A04 and 2023 Angèle Rouge. It is thus a great joy to have with us Ninon Lomenech and Ursula Townsend and their families.

'Sadly, Julia Garnett and Jean-Jacques Tremayne could not join us, but I do know that they are very proud of John and Jean-Jacques. JJ was Commanding Officer of 2023 for several operations. He was a very brave man and a splendid seaman – and I commend him to you.

'Of course, the many missions would not have been possible without our marvellous crews. They were nearly all fishermen, and they were not only sea salts, but the salt of the earth as well. You could not fault any of them. I know that both

Sir Brooks and Lady Richards leaving the unveiling ceremony.

Paul O'Brien addresses the assembled company from a rowing boat in New Grimsby.

Daniel (Lomenech) and Richard (Townsend) would like me to remember and savour especially Jasper Lawn, Ralph Hockney (their two Coxswains) and Cookie Nash who kept us all alive with his amazing meals, come hell or high water.

'If we could not have managed without these men, nor could we have coped without our back-up team, of whom, first of all, was Captain Frank Slocum – DDODI, a Director of the SIS. His brilliant staff officer and immaculate planner Steven Mackenzie, and Nigel Warrington-Smyth, Senior Officer Inshore Patrol. This was our nomme de plume – or nomme de guerre – and he kept us hard at it, as well as at our other activities.*

'Our dear late friend Captain Tommy Tucker of the Royal Corps of Signals was our radio king who fitted us out with some remarkable radio equipment, and among many unheralded people serving on* Sunbeam II *in Helford was her Wireless Officer, David Herbert, who kept watch for us with unswerving commitment.*

'If Braiden Rock marked our departure, it was also our point of return to the genuine warmth, hospitality and kindness of the people of Tresco. Above all, we would like to thank and salute them for keeping 'mum' for so long, and so successfully!*

'I know the crews would have liked me to mention without fail John Williams of the New Inn and his wife who did so much to sustain their morale!*

"Thus the plaque I will now unveil – it is not only for the ships, but will be a lasting memento and symbol of the continuing bond between us, our friends here, and all Scillonians.*

'Vive La France!*

'Vive les Bretons!*

'Vive Grand Bretagne!'*

Sir Brooks Richards in Brittany, 2002.

That evening we had a dinner in a private dining room at the Island Hotel on Tresco. It was quiet, but full of thoughtful conversation and good company. During the course of the evening, General Sir Michael Rose – himself a member of the Special Forces, former head of the SAS and commander of Allied Forces in Bosnia – made a comment that I have never forgotten. "What these men did, and the plans that they were able to retrieve and bring back to Tresco probably saved half a million lives in the D-Day landings."

It was a great honour to have been part of the commemoration, to have been amongst heroes and to have learned something of the secret war of which Tresco was part sixty years ago.

The plaque that we unveiled at Braiden Rock is a short walk from the quay shop in New Grimsby. Take the cliff path along the harbour that starts behind the shop. After 200 metres you will be faced by a steep outcrop of rock. To your left is a short path down to the sea. At the bottom – about 30 metres – is a worn set of steps from which they embarked. On the rock next to the steps is the plaque. It's quite a private place, and you have to work a little to find it – but that, I think, is as it should be.

You can read much more detail and more first-hand accounts of the secret sea-line to Occupied France in Sir Brooks Richard's own history of Special Forces *Secret Flotillas* that is soon to be republished. While researching this story for the *Tresco Times*, I came across an anomaly: Special Forces officers on

Tresco frequently appeared in photographs under different names. One in particular, Jean-Jacques Tremayne also appears as J-J Allen. I queried this with Sir Brooks Richards. This was his reply:

The Angele Rouge *at speed.*

'The picture of Angele Rouge MFV2023 *showing the tricolor on the ship's bows were taken in New Grimsby on her return from an operation with J-J Allen in command. He's the small fellow looking over the bulwarks. He is also the chap in civilian clothes in the group of officers which includes Lord David Herbert and Nigel Warrington-Smyth (partly effaced for security). The picture of the ship taken from the air shows her at speed during an operation.*

'The designer of 2023 was Jack Laurent Giles, then working in the Director of Naval Constructors Office in Bath. J-J Allen and Jean-Jacques Tremayne are one and the same person. French Naval Officers who joined the Royal Navy after the fall of France were in double jeopardy. Like de Gaulle himself, they might be condemned to death in absentia by Court Martial in France, but they were also violently disliked by the Gaullists who considered that all patriotic Frenchmen ought to join the Free French Forces. Hence their adoption of British pseudonyms.

'J-J's original surname was Gilbert, but presumably, after his stay in Cornwall, he preferred to adopt "Tremayne" rather than the "Allen" given him by the RN in 1940 when he became one of the officers in Fidelity. *He was one of the very few survivors when that ship was lost with over 400 crew.'*

J-J Allen in civilian clothes.

But perhaps the last word in this curious and hitherto secret chapter of naval history, in which Tresco was part, belongs to 'Remy'. Their trip to Tresco was not without tragedy. One of the two Beaufighters that had escorted them into British waters crashed with the loss of both the crew while flying low over the boat.

'I have saved this piece of paper, torn from a pad headed 'Naval Message', scribbled in pencil with all the mistakes, so moving when one thinks of the friendship which unites pilots. I thought of those two lads, very young, (I have since learned that they were brothers) setting out this morning on what they thought was a pleasure trip, and who had undoubtedly wished to entertain my children with their aerobatics, and who had met their death under a clear sky which merged with the calm blue sea. I have also saved three pieces of aluminium, which had broken off from the undercarriage when it was hoisted on to the deck.

Jean-Claude Renault, son of 'Remy' in Brittany 2002.

'A friend in France being tortured to make him give away the secret of the place where I had hidden my family – two airmen abruptly snatched from life when they had come to protect us – and our young friend de Beaufort (Leger) who had accompanied us at the start of our adventurous voyage by taking us in his vehicle, and who was shot by the Germans on the very eve of the Liberation.

'When my children are much older, I will explain to them what their own lives are worth and how much had been paid for them, the debts they owe to all those people to justify so many sacrifices.'

The crest of U-boat U-681.

THE WRECK OF U-BOAT *U-681*

Divers may have located the wreck of German submarine *U-681* near the Bishop Rock. She was built at Hamburg in 1944 (67.1 metres overall, 1,070 tons) and she belonged to 11 Flotille – a Frontflotille (Combat Flotilla) based in Norway.

Her commander, Werner Gebauer, struck a rock while submerged in Broad Sound on 10 March 1945. Unable to stay underwater, *U-681* attempted a surface passage to a neutral port in Ireland. But she was sunk the next day at 0930 by a Liberator bomber of VPB-103 Squadron, 7th Fleet Air Wing US Navy, based at Dunkeswell, Devon. 11 of the crew of *U-681* were killed and 38 survivors captured.

HMS *HOOD*

HMS *Hood*, on a visit to Scilly shortly before she was sunk by the *Bismarck* with the loss of all but three of her ship's company.

CHAPTER FIFTEEN
TRESCO AGRICULTURAL SHOW

When the Second World War finished in 1945, many communities in Britain looked for ways to cheer themselves up and celebrate the peace following years of deprivation. Tresco was no exception, and at the Major's suggestion Agricultural Shows were organised and were received on the island with much enthusiasm.

By enhancing these small black-and-white snaps taken at these shows it is possible to pick out details. Characters jump from the page. What an extraordinary time it must have been. Look closely at the photos. Everyone was involved and everyone was there to enjoy themselves.

The Show was open not just to Tresco residents but also to other islands, and they all entered into the spirit of the event with just as much enthusiasm as the Tresco.

Ralph Whitlock came to judge the exhibits and present the prizes. Ralph was himself a farmer and a national broadcaster on the radio, listened to every week by millions.

Meanwhile on Bryher, they had a Jersey cow thought to be the equal of anything in Tresco's famous herd. The only problem was how to get it there for the show.

Islanders are resourceful and practical, particularly the Jenkins family. They had a boat and they had a cow, and so they put the two together and solved the problem.

Fortunately, someone was there with a camera to capture the moment that Bryher's best cow came to the show. The small boy in the picture is Kenny

Tresco farmers bring their prize animals to the show.

'Cattle and flowers appeared to be the future'.

Cow, boat. Boat, cow...

Cow embarks...

Cow at sea...

Cow arrives safely...

Ralph Whitlock addresses the islanders, before presenting the prizes.

Jenkins. Today he looks more like the HMS *Hero* sailor on the old Players' cigarette packet, and is one of the skippers and owners of the *Firethorn*, flagship of the islands' boat service.

The Bryher men were not alone in shipping livestock by open boat. It was a fairly normal way to ship cows, and in one rescue from a shipwreck – the *Minnehaha* – the Bryher gig had rescued a herd from the wreckage by swimming them to shore beside the gig.

By all accounts these shows were a great success and raised the spirits and morale of the islanders in the austere 50s. It must have been a difficult time rebuilding a small community after so many families had been separated from their fathers who were away fighting. A great deal of the old community 'togetherness' was once again established, as Tresco looked forward to a future that was thought to be agricultural rather than touristic. Cattle and flowers appeared to be the future.

The photographs below open a window on another world. Here is the presentation ceremony, presided over by the Major. Radio celebrity Ralph Whitlock has judged the exhibits and will present the prizes. The famous

broadcaster addresses the islanders who gather round expectantly. On the blackboard the name of the Cups and the winners have been carefully chalked.

The late 40s were a time of austerity, but everyone still made the effort to dress up. Women wore printed summer dresses and hats, men jackets, and quite often ties and hats. Your clothes were still, in those days, a statement of your status. So what then do we make of Rodney Ward, receiving his prize dressed in tennis clothes?

Closer inspection of the blackboard behind him, show that he is receiving the Cornish Riviera Cup.

Rodney Ward receives his prize dressed in tennis clothes.

Judging by the blackboard, it was a good day for the Major – with either himself or his wife winning half the prizes. Also listed as a winner is Mrs A Oyler, wife of the tenant farmer up at Borough in the middle of the island. Today the Oyler family still occupy the farm.

It seems to have been a day of bucolic enjoyment, straight from the pages of the *Darling Buds of May*, everyone smiling and everyone knowing just where they stood in the community. A good time was had by all. Tresco is back together after the war, a small island once again at peace with itself.

Coronation Day on Tresco, 1952.

The Major was held in great affection. He was the head of a feudal system that carried responsibilities on all sides. Estate workers were expected to work hard and loyally for the Estate, in return they could expect a paternalistic concern for their well-being, employment for life and a house for them and their spouse until death.

This cradle-to-grave system only worked if there was respect on both sides, and this was the key to success. It was such an English concept. Other countries had revolutions, and could never understand why the English workingman accepted a landed class who were so enormously privileged.

These pictures, taken shortly after the Second World War, show a way of life that was still being enacted in villages all over England.

In 1952, the Queen was crowned and Tresco responded with a big party which included the decoration of the island carriage.

CHAPTER SIXTEEN
SHIPWRECK! – THE *MANDO*

Lifeboat Coxswain Matt Lethbridge Senior was awarded a Bronze Medal for the rescue of the crew of the *Mando*...

On St Mary's, 'Boy' Matt heard the steamer blowing loud. She had to be very close indeed he reckoned. After a while, the sound stopped. "She's either gone away, or she's aground" he joked to Jimmy Jenkins, Bo'sun of the *Scillonian*.

Within minutes, they knew the truth when 'Boy's' father, who had been alerted by the Coastguard, found him. "She's aground" said Matt senior "Come on...!"

They launched the St Mary's lifeboat at 9 pm at nearly low water which forced her to take the long passage in the darkness and fog past Samson and White Island, through Castle Bryher Neck, between Gweal and Scilly Rock, then round the top of Bryher. They thought the *Mando* was on Men a Vaur because that's what the men at Round Island Light believed – not being able to see in the fog. Just before she struck, the *Mando* had erroneously given her position as 87 miles west of the Bishop (probably from her noonday fix).

Then through the darkness the lifeboatmen saw the glow of a fire that the *Mando* crew had lit on her aft deck.

The *Mando* sailors had lowered their boats, filled them with their possessions, and were about to board them from ladders hung from the superstructure in the *Mando*.

The Mando *aground.*

The Mando *aground.*

"Get on board and stop them, or someone's going to get hurt in this swell" Matt senior told his son. So 'Boy' leapt aboard, found the Italian Captain and persuaded him by sign language to bring his men down to the deck where they could jump into the Lifeboat. Matt senior skillfully kept station in a heavy swell with the engines. 'Boy' helped the Captain collect his papers, before they both left the stricken ship – the last to get off.

They then took crew's luggage, in tow. They returned through New Grimsby Channel, and while waiting for the tide they transferred the crew's belongings into the lifeboat, leaving the ship's boats to the Bryher men who had put out in a launch. Soon the fog lifted and the lifeboat finally returned to St Mary's at a little after midnight. Another job well done.

Next day, 'Boy' returned with the Italian captain in a small boat to try and get aboard and retrieve the Log, but the *Mando* had already been swamped and the mass of water ebbing and flowing through the scuttles made any return too dangerous. The sea had claimed her, and she was starting to break up.

A NIGHT TO REMEMBER OF TRESCO

Dear Editor

Perhaps you would like to print my account of the 1955 wreck of the 'Mando' in your paper. The events of that night will bring back memories to your older readers.

Yours sincerely

John C Harding   Exmouth

'Although the official record of the wreck of the Mando *states she was on a voyage from Hampton Roads, USA to Ymuiden with a cargo of coal dust, it was generally known on Scilly that she was from South Africa bound for Holland and – based on her last position and heading – this seems likely. I hope so, since many hours were spent on her after she was wrecked looking for smuggled diamonds!*

'The fog on 21 January 1955 was the thickest I have encountered. So dense was it, that the sound of the Round Island foghorn could not be heard on Tresco. But the surf of St Helen's Bar could be heard as a constant roar – fog always 'lifts' the height of the groundswell, something I've never been able to fathom out.

'A steamer was 'blowing' to the west of Bryher, the deep sound of a large vessel which echoed through the islands. There was a throatiness about it, a sound of command: "I am here get out of my way". She had been there all afternoon slowly moving NE. After tea I went to see Ted Eveleigh who was in his greenhouse with Clarence Handy listening to the marine frequency on a short-wave radio.

'We were joined by Bill Gibbons, Sammy Bond, Fred Richards and Frank Naylor – forty years on I still remember the names of all who lived on Tresco, and yet I cannot remember names of work colleagues from 5 years ago!

'A steamer was talking on Ted's radio... it was the **Mando**. She was loud and clear, so when she gave her position as 280 nautical miles west of Ushant we had our doubts. These doubts must have been shared by Land's End Radio who gave a radio fix.

'As the ship's radio operator was talking we could hear the whistle blow over the radio, and 10-15 seconds later the sound reached us. The steamer had to be the Mando and she was less than half a mile from Bolt Head. This information was passed on the phone by Ted Eveleigh to St Mary's Coastguard.

'We were later told that the **Mando** saw Round Island through the fog, heard the foghorn, mistook it for a large vessel, went hard a'starboard and full ahead – straight onto St Helen's Bar.

'The five short blasts on her whistle could be heard throughout the islands.

'Everyone on Scilly knew that a large steamer was aground to the north. On St Mary's the lifeboat was launched. On Bryher, brave men put to sea in a gig. Today, gigs are in regular use and are seaworthy, but in 1955 the gig Sussex that was used that night had not been in the water for years. She must have 'opened up' and leaked like a basket, but launch her they did.

'On St Martin's there was someone with leadership and initiative. They took life-saving equipment, landed on St Helen's and made their way across the island to the Bar – the very area where help would have been needed if the crew had taken to the boats.

'On Tresco, Bill Gibbons led the way. He considered taking his boat The **Canadian** to the area where it was thought the **Mando** might be. He asked for volunteers to go with him. Now Bill was a fine boatman, the best, I would have gone anywhere with him – despite the fact that he would make a temporary repair to his Kelvin engine with a piece of string, and a more permanent one with a piece of wire!

'Harry Clement was the first to step forward. Frank Naylor and myself followed. However, we had only a limited knowledge of the area and Bill wanted someone with more experience. So there was a change of plan...

'About six of us made our way to Piper's Hole. The fog was thicker than ever – then by a miracle it lifted for a few moments to a height of about thirty feet.

'Suddenly we could see flares, search lights and then the port and starboard lights of a large vessel.

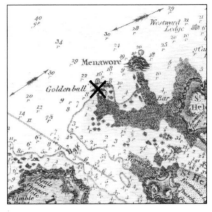

X marks the spot where the **Mando** *was wrecked. Detail from Graeme Spence's Survey.*

'Someone produced a powerful torch, my RAF service would come in useful!

"Do you receive me?" I flashed.

'The Radio Officer on **Mando** *was quick off the mark*

"Stop, Stop, Rocks, go to starboard, come astern!" He had mistaken me for another ship.

"Lifeboat on way, help on way" I flashed. The fog was returning. "Do you understand?"

"Yes. Thank you. Thank you" With that the fog came down again.

'Someone, Pete Locke I think, ran back to Ted Eveleigh who relayed the above to St Mary's.

'Later the lifeboat reported that all the crew had been taken off and that they had the Bryher gig in tow. Then with a laugh "and she's full of coal dust!"

WELCOME BACK!

For one of the seamen rescued from the *Mando* it must have seemed all too familiar.

On 27 October 1927 – 28 years before – another Italian ship, the SS *Isabo*, struck Scilly Rock in dense fog. In one of the most heroic rescues in Scillonian history 32 of her crew were saved and 6 perished.

One of the heroes that night was Matt Lethbridge senior, coxswain of the St Mary's lifeboat. One of those he saved was the young pantry-boy of the *Isabo* who was found clinging to the rigging.

On 21 January 1955 this most unfortunate fellow was once again wrecked in the fog on Scilly in the *Mando* – a mile and a half from his first wreck – and again he was rescued by the same lifeboat under the same coxswain – Matt Lethbridge senior.

Matt Lethbridge today.

The *Mando*. *Painted by Matt 'Boy' Lethbridge.*

CHAPTER SEVENTEEN

TOM DORRIEN SMITH 1913–1973

Proprietor from 1955

In 1955 the Major was succeeded by his son Tom Dorrien Smith. Tom had retired from the Navy, and was usually known as 'The Commander.'

Once again, it was time for a change of emphasis if the island was to survive as a private island in the austerity years after the war. The Commander had inherited a Garden that was now attracting seventeen thousand paying visitors a year. However it did not generate enough revenue to sustain the team of gardeners and the inherent maintenance costs.

Elsewhere on the island he had a substantial stock of cottages and farm buildings that could be used as holiday accommodation.

The Commander made a decision; he would share his lovely island with visitors who would pay to holiday there. Three years after he inherited Tresco, he selected a small number of cottages to be used for holiday letting during the summer. They were simple island cottages with basic facilities, but they proved extremely popular.

Tom Dorrien Smith.

Farming scenes on Tresco.

The Island Hotel in the 1960s.

Flower packing on Tresco.

Two years later, the Commander felt confident enough to convert and enlarge some old coastguard cottages in Old Grimsby into the Island Hotel. It opened for business in 1960.

The Commander's decision meant that Tresco had taken its first steps towards becoming a tourist destination for a limited number of people, and in doing so had secured the future of the island community and – of course – the Abbey Gardens.

The Commander was married to the Georgian Princess, Tamara Imeritinsky, who bore him five children – Teona, Alexandra, Robert, Charlotte and James. All the family were expected to take a close interest in the Garden and all took part in the practical work of maintaining it.

The Commander was elected as Chairman of the Isles of Scilly Council – unlike his forbears who inherited the office by right of birth. The family continued to exert considerable, and now democratic, influence over all the islands.

Under his leadership, the Tresco Abbey Garden continued to expand as new species were introduced. In 1963 the Commander took his mother, Eleanor, on a trip retracing her 1909 honeymoon trip to Australia. They returned with a mass of rare plants collected from the major botanic gardens on the eastern Australian coast with which to enrich the Abbey Garden.

The Commander enjoyed telling the Tresco story with enthusiasm and vivid descriptions – whether he was lecturing the Royal Horticultural Society or talking to friends. He lived a life committed to Tresco, and always took a leading part in island activities.

He died in 1973. His son Robert inherited, aged 22, while still at university.

Eddie Birch remembers May Day 50 years ago:

'We had the donkey cart all decorated up. The May Queen was crowned on the School Green, and then we'd have a procession up to the Abbey. The babies would sit in the donkey cart with the great iron wheels, and the mothers followed behind. We'd sing some songs up there and then go to every house, sing a song, take a few handfuls of gorse petals – that the mothers had collected from the Downs – and sprinkle it for luck on the doorstep. Then down to the Farm for lunch, and carry on round the island.

'The eldest boy always led the procession, carrying a Union Jack. I was once the eldest boy when my sister Jean was the May Queen. It was all just a good bit of fun to us.'

Islander Eddie Birch today.

May Day in the 50s. Eddie Birch is nearest the camera.

New Grimsby Quay

The Island Fete was always enjoyed by everyone. Local produce was available without rationing, and there was often a band.

Coal was brought to the island by a coaling ship that had to be unloaded at New Grimsby Quay.

Ned Steele – the cobbler – and Emma.

Gloria Terry in the 50s. Gloria still works on the island in the Quay Shop.

Gloria, Pete Locke and Nonie Handy – all still on the island today.

Gloria gets married.

LETTERS

Dear Editor

As a teenager in the early 50s I lodged with Emma and Ned Steele when I worked in the Estate Office. The enclosed photograph is of Emma and Ned at their gate. Emma had a budgie which was partial to a drop of beer when Ned came home from an evening at the New Inn. The budgie was poorly and Emma prepared a shoe box lined with moss for a burial. However she was advised to give the budgie some grass, so the box was put back in the shed and the budgie survived to entertain us for a while longer.

One day a neighbour asked if Emma and Ned had cast out. No, said I (thinking, nosey beggar!). "Well" he said "when they are talking, his pyjamas and her nightdress hang together on the line. If they had cast out they hung at each end of the line!"

Happy days!

JEAN ELLIOTT
(née Harding)

Kelso, Scotland

Dear Editor

... it brought back memories of Ned, working in his Cobbler's shop and sticking the huge leather needles into his wooden leg. As a little girl, when I tried this on my own leg, with a darning needle, my father explained that cobblers had wooden legs especially to hold their needles!

Yours nostalgically

GLENYS MACKIE
(née Venn)

Llangammarch Wells, Powys

The Queen Mother and the Commander.

The Queen Mother with the Commander at the Monument on Tresco.

The Queen Mother meets the school-children. The two children bowing to each other rather than Royalty are not confused – they are part of a May Day dance.

A visit from Her Majesty, Prince Philip and Prince Charles.

CHAPTER EIGHTEEN

ROBERT DORRIEN SMITH 1951 –

Proprietor from 1973

Robert and Lucy Dorrien Smith.

For nearly two centuries the Dorrien Smith family has nurtured and supported the community of Tresco. Back in 1834 Augustus Smith wanted to create a utopia based around Jeremy Bentham's concept that "the greatest happiness of the greatest number is the foundation of morals and legislation." Both men believed in "enlightened self-interest" in that people who acted for their own maximum satisfaction would, in the long run, always act rightly.

As the last quarter of the 20th century approached, Tresco's small community appeared to be a living and successful example of Benthamism. However it had been at a cost, and most of it had fallen on the Dorrien Smiths.

Robert inherited Tresco in 1973 on the death of his father, Tom. A year later Harold Wilson's second Labour government was elected with the declared intention of 'squeezing the rich until the pips squeaked'. Owners of large private estates were now squarely in the firing line. Only a creative solution could possibly save the way of life that islanders enjoyed.

A scheme was devised for some of the islands holiday cottages based on a Swiss concept that had been created in ski resorts. The idea was to offer a lease on a property for just the time that holidaymakers wanted to use it – rather than selling them the whole property. This idea of several people sharing time in a holiday property became known as 'timeshare' and became an affordable way for people to own their holiday.

In 1978, Tresco created its first timeshare cottages – and they were immediately successful. Capital could be raised without losing control, the holidaymakers were guaranteed a reservation each year, and Tresco was certain of full cottages every year.

Still in his twenties 'Mr Robert', as he was known to islanders, was in charge of an island community that looked to him for leadership and their future security.

Private islands get few grants, and Tresco had to become financially self-sufficient. Gradually the team was built, and standards were raised. The Island Hotel that his father had created was extended, more cottages were converted to holiday letting.

Environmental projects on Tresco also benefited; the reeds were cleared around the Great Pool to create a wetland for migratory birds, a private sewage system was installed to keep the waters around Tresco clear and unpolluted. In 1987 the old engine house was closed. No longer would the island generate its own electricity, Tresco was connected to the mains. Suddenly unheard of luxuries such as washing machines and dishwasher could be used.

The island was back on its feet for the benefit of both islanders and visitors alike.

A direct helicopter link with Penzance was opened up in 1983, making the island more accessible.

The Gardens were savaged again by a snow storm in 1987 and then by a hurricane in 1990. Again the gardeners were called on to restore and replant. The result was magnificent. They looked on the positive side and found new areas of sheltered sunshine in which to plant, while gradually replacing the damaged shelter-belt.

Together, Robert and Lucy Dorrien Smith created a private collection of modern art by West Country artists and others who have been inspired by the islands. Gallery Tresco was opened to encourage and promote local artists and craftsmen.

Tresco Children by David Wynne.

Two fine sculptures by David Wynne were positioned in the Gardens. 'Tresco Children', modelled on Robert's own children, is positioned at the lower end of the Gardens at the end of an important vista. Gaia is modelled on David Wynne's wife Gill. The beautifully striated South African marble block from which it is shaped was considered too difficult to be carved. Beatle George Harrison bought it and gave it to David Wynne as a challenge. He was right. David Wynne eventually created a masterpiece.

When Augustus Smith came to Scilly in 1834 he lifted the island communities out of poverty and encouraged enlightened self interest amongst islanders. Those who wanted to help themselves were given the means and encouragement to do so. This was not understood by his peers on the mainland. But he stood alone and prospered.

His descendants Thomas, Arthur, Tom and Robert, have each built upon the foundations laid by Augustus. Each inherited some problems, each found their own solution, and every time the community has benefited.

Today Tresco remains a paternalistic community, but one in which islanders are encouraged to show initiative and enterprise, where pensioners are housed free after retirement, where the Proprietor is benevolent and where the employees are fiercely loyal. It may be old-fashioned, out of fashion even, but it could be the best form of society there is. Certainly hundreds of visitors are attracted every year to relish for a short while a quality of life that can no longer be found on the mainland.

Gaia.

The next generation of Dorrien Smiths is represented by Adam, Frances and Michael from Robert's first marriage to Lady Emma Windsor Clive, and by Marina and Tristan from his marriage to Lucy Morgan Smith.

ROYAL VISITS

The Queen Mother was a frequent visitor, and as a keen gardener, took a close interest in the Gardens.

The Queen Mother in the Gardens.

The Queen Mother arrives at Old Grimsby, June 1985.

The Queen Mother enjoyed a short trip in the tractor-drawn bus.

The Prince and Princess of Wales at Tresco.

Prince Charles and Diana, pregnant with William, visited Scilly in the early eighties. They also paid a private visit in 1992. It was to be their last holiday together. The following weekend Andrew Morton's book was released and their problems became public property.

CHAPTER NINETEEN
BIRTH OF THE *TRESCO TIMES*

O n our first day on Tresco, when Kathy and I took that walk amid the Bronze Age graves on the North End it was the start of a new chapter and a kind of initiation. After 11 years on Tresco, I now realise what a special place we had chosen for our midday nap that first day.

On Tresco the veil between the after-life and the world in which we live is at its thinnest and most translucent. Give yourself up to the land, let the island take over and you will plug into an extraordinary sensation: time seems to disappear. Remove time and you are among your ancestors. This is why the North End is a sacred place and was considered so by our earliest predecessors who chose to bury their dead here. Walk the North End of Tresco yourself and see if it's true.

The number of Bronze Age graves on Scilly is out of all proportion to the likely contemporary population of the islands. Bodies of warriors or chieftains must have been ferried here from the mainland to lie in this sacred spot.

So we lay on the heather at the wild North End of Tresco in a dream-world between sleep and wakefulness, as the shades tiptoed around us.

The lack of a sense of time on has been remarked by many Tresco visitors; past and present merge, and childhood seems like yesterday.

Lying there, my mind drifted back to my early years... to when I was three years-old. I had a special friend then, the same age as me, who could do things of which I could only dream. Driving a double-decker bus down our muddy farm lane, piloting aeroplanes or just knowing where the deepest and muddiest puddles were. Although no one else ever saw him, he was my best friend.

The North End.

These reminiscences rolled through my mind as I lay on the heather at the North End of Tresco half a century later. For a moment I had been magicked back to early childhood.

I opened my eyes; a figure in a roll-neck sweater, was smoking a pipe reflectively and smiling. My friend was back and Tresco was going to suit him right down to the ground. He had become 'The Commodore'.

A spot of rain fell. Unnoticed, a black cloud had piled up behind us. Another drop fell. Soon it would be a downpour. Kathy and I jumped up and we started to run back for home...

THE BIRTH OF THE *TRESCO TIMES*
The Estate Office is situated in the middle of the island, and in 1991 it contained just a handful of workers. Upstairs, Robert Dorrien Smith sat like the captain on the bridge with a good view of the road outside. In an office next to him sat his personal assistant, the redoubtable Eve Cooper. Eve

Early editions of the Tresco Times.

combined efficiency, tact, attention to detail and charm in equal proportions. She is married to Roy, Tresco's former Postmaster and amateur historian.

From his elevated office, Robert watched the comings and goings of the island while he worked. Almost everyone, islander or visitor, came to the Estate Office at least once during the week.

Downstairs, two accountant-cum-book-keepers worked in the back office and Wendy Gleadle and I occupied the front. We were the Cottage Department and Tourist Information Centre on Tresco.

Wendy and Ron, her husband, had come to Tresco at least a decade before me. Ron was a doctor and an eye specialist who had chosen to down-size his life long before this had become as fashionable as it is today. Leaving behind the stress of his professional career, he was a valued member of the gardening team in the Abbey Garden. This gave him the time to pursue the passion of

ISSUE NO. 1 **SPRING 1991**

TRESCO · TIMES

Welcome to the first issue of TRESCO TIMES

This newsletter is being produced as a result of many requests from both residents and holiday visitors. We hope you enjoy the first copy, and that it may stimulate you to take up your pen and write to the Editor with a contribution for the next issue. We would love to hear from islanders and visitors with news, views, comments, memories, poems, advertisements, etc.

Contributions should be sent to the Editor, Mrs. Wendy Gleadle, Tresco Estate Office, Isles of Scilly, Cornwall, TR24 0QQ.
(Telephone 0720 22849)

My thanks to all contributors to this first issue. In particular I am grateful to Mr. Robert Dorrien-Smith for his advice and help and the following articles on this page. Many visitors to the Abbey Garden over the past eighteen months have been intrigued by the two new statues "Gaia" and "Tresco Children". They are both the work of the world-renowned sculptor, David Wynne, and I am most grateful to him for his interesting article on the background of how "Gaia" came to be created.

Mr. Robert Dorrien-Smith

from Robert Dorrien-Smith ......
Woodland Restoration

Following the devastation of the January 1990 hurricane, we have now formulated and agreed a five-year clearance and replanting plan and engaged mainland contractors to carry out the work.

"Making a start on the Woodland Clearance"

Owing to the number and size of fallen trees and the difficulties of transporting the heavy machinery required, it will be several years before the full effects of this work are visible. However, it is vital that we re-establish the shelter belts to protect the Abbey Garden and in the early stages of the contract we will be concentrating on replanting Abbey Hill. Hopefully, each year will see substantial changes in the woodland landscape.

Good News on Sewage!

For the last three years the Estate has been investigating the possibility of grant aid towards an island sewage scheme that would enable us to remove the outfalls from the various beaches round the island. Sadly, the Government's interest in a cleaner environment for us all appears to be more political than practical, and our negotiations with the Department of the Environment and others for grants have been unsuccessful.

However, I judge the issue to be of great long-term importance to the business and the community and have therefore decided to proceed with a scheme which provides for the collection and treatment of sewage from all parts of the island, except one or two isolated properties with septic tanks, with the treated effluent being discharged from a long

Fine Screening Plant

"One of the biggest civil works projects ever undertaken on the island"

sea outfall to the north of the Island Hotel.

This is one of the biggest civil works projects ever undertaken on the Island, and during the winter we have had trenches and mounds of earth all over the island. The work was completed in late February and the outfalls on Pentle Bay, New Grimsby Channel and Old Grimsby beaches are now all obsolete. Hopefully this will have a beneficial effect both on the bathing beaches and the marine environment.

Roads & Sea Defences

Having rebuilt the Appletree sea defences during the summer of 1990, work continues at a number of sites on the island; in particular the Quay Shop, which was nearly swept away in the gales. You will also notice a new road from Penzance Gate to Rowesfield Cottages. In addition, many of the old roads were in a very bad state of repair, and several sections have been broken up and replaced. We also hope to include within the contract, if time permits, improvements to landscaping around the new Estate yard at New Grimsby.

his life – watching the wonderful bird-life for which Scilly, and Tresco in particular, is renowned. He also instituted his popular Sunday morning bird-walks that were always accompanied by his erudite commentary.

Wendy introduced me to the ways of the Cottage Department. All bookings and reservations were kept in great ledgers that were constantly up-dated with pencil and eraser. It was a cumbersome system, but it worked. Such was the popularity of Tresco holiday cottages that mostly the same people re-booked and came back again the following year. From this developed the concept of Tresco Timeshare that I had helped set up with Robert in 1978. Timesharers made a payment in advance to own a particular holiday week in their favourite cottage.

My job was to take over the running of the timeshare and to expand it. The timeshare department had been run on the back of an envelope, with hand-written notes and letters typed by whoever could be found to fit in the work. The front office had one electric typewriter.

I asked for a computer. This was duly delivered, although loaded with an archaic word-processing programme that reduced the computer's capability to little more than a simple word processor. Still, it was a start.

Most of the potential customers for timeshare were either cottage renters, or guests at the Island Hotel or New Inn. We decided that they should be written to on a regular basis – a quarterly newsletter.

The idea was to write about life on the island, to bring them Tresco when they were not there. We wanted to give them a year-round view of the island.

Wendy was enthusiastic, and had got there before me. She had started a newsletter called The *Tresco Times* a year before. She wrote it all, before sending it to the printers to design and lay it out. We agreed that our new newsletter would continue the name – The *Tresco Times*.

Wendy graciously, although I suspect reluctantly, ceded the editorship and thus began ten years of the *Tresco Times*. It now has a print-run in excess of 40,000 and is mailed out to 36 countries around the world. It remains a selective and personal view of the island and its inhabitants.

Here are some extracts from stories that we covered over the years:

Insular Things 1

TV STAR BECOMES A CURATOR

You might have thought that there is no higher position in the Abbey Garden than Head Gardener. But this is not the case. Mike "Where's the Camera?" Nelhams has been appointed Curator in recognition of his outstanding work not only in the Garden itself but also in liaising with other famous Gardens throughout the world. The new position underlines the importance of the Abbey Garden in the wider world of international Botany. Everyone congratulates Mike on his new status as the Gardens' first-ever Curator.

Of course, regular readers will remember Mike's famous statement in one of his many television appearances that he wasn't really "a wheelbarrow and wellies sort of gardener", and will realise that he was actually a Curator all along. He will now have more time to lecture and to travel on plant-collecting trips around the world.

Curator Mike Nelhams

This of course, means that someone has to fill the gap while Mike carries out his additional duties. Step forward, Chief Propagator Andrew Lawson.

Andrew has been promoted to Garden Supervisor in recognition of his sterling work over many years. Our congratulations to him, as well.

Only one question is left. Will Mike's designer stubble remain? Is this the image of the new younger breed of Curator? We'll let you know.

TOP FLIGHT   Summer 1996

Years ago when the earth was young, the Editor was a naval officer cadet at BRNC Dartmouth. Sadly, Her Majesty dispensed with his services before he could show his mettle as a real naval officer.

However, others of his year rose to greater heights – and one in particular became Very Important Indeed, commanding our flagship *Ark Royal* in the

recent naval blockade of Bosnia – even appearing on television news to explain to the nation what was happening over there. The Editor wrote to him – as one does when a classmate succeeds at something – and in due course a reply arrived from the Admiral, with an invitation to dinner. Not just any dinner, but a full-blown reunion of those who had served the Senior Service in a more distinguished way than the Editor. A Search and Rescue helicopter which happened to be exercising off Scilly on the appointed day diverted to Tresco to pick up the Editor and whisk him to RNAS Culdrose in Cornwall where the dinner was held.

So it was that the officer cadet, Royal Navy (retired) sat down with the Admiral, and many tales of youthful escapades were exchanged over a good Malt, and undying friendship sworn before the Great Man flew off to distant lands on affairs of State. Which all goes to show that there is nothing as satisfying as friendship renewed, and nothing as generous as naval hospitality.

SPRING 1994

When a schoolmaster at Venture Academy in the village of Joe Batt's Arm on Fogo Island – 3,500 miles away in Newfoundland – set his class of 10 year-olds a project last year, he little realised that it would occupy column inches in the *Tresco Times*. Along with the rest of the class, pupil Michelle Furlong placed a letter in a bottle and launched it into the sea. Five months later, it turned up on Tresco – almost exactly due East – where it was found by RCI visitor Mrs Cox.

To whom it may concern:

My name is Michelle Furlong, I am 10 years old. I attend grade five at Venture Academy, Fogo Island. This is a school project that my class is doing. I am hoping that someone will find this bottle and write me at the following address.

Thank you.

Michelle Furlong (age 10)
PO Box S2
Joe Batt's Arm
Fogo Island
Newfoundland A06 2X0
CANADA

This was followed by a letter in our next edition:

Dear Editor

I thought you might be interested to put a note in the Tresco Times *about the letter in a bottle that was found on the island in February sent by Michelle Furlong of Joe Batt's Arm, Fogo Island, Newfoundland.*

My husband was born on an island off the north east coast of Newfoundland not far from Fogo Island, so when he read in the Tresco Times *about the letter while on holiday in May, he decided that he would like to see Michelle when next in Newfoundland.*

On 15 September we went by ferry to Fogo Island and drove to Joe Batt's Arm. We were able to find Mr and Mrs Furlong as it is a small fishing village of about 1,400 people. We saw Michelle when she came out of school and she was so

pleased to meet us, especially as I was English and spoke differently. She was a sweet girl with a lovely family and I am going to keep in touch with them.

It was certainly a strange co-incidence that the bottle should have been sent from an island and then found on an island over here. We hope to visit Tresco again next year.

Yours faithfully

Mrs BC Abbott
Horley, Surrey

MURDER FILE CLOSED

Cornwall Police closed the files on a St Martin's murder case, after forensic explained that the body was over 3,000 years old.

NURSES AVAILABLE FOR TIMESHARE!

Great headline... but not perhaps what you hoped. Nurses – a cosy period cottage, once the residence of the island's registered nurse, is now available for timeshare.

SOCIAL NICETIES

Overheard on Tresco: a mother with 'cool' teenage son.

Son (Embarrassed): Mum, you keep saying "hello" to everyone.

Mother: I know, isn't it lovely. People on Tresco are so friendly.

Son (Explaining): But Mum, you keep saying "hello" first...

...AND FROM THE ACCOUNTS DEPARTMENT

Absolutely nothing unusual or exciting has happened in the Accounts Department lately. Good news, surely?

CHAPTER TWENTY
WINTER ON TRESCO

A DIFFERENT SORT OF WINTER VISITOR

Winter on Tresco is a magical time. For three months from mid November until mid February the island reverts to being a small community with few visitors. It is a breathing space that is needed.

Not the usual funny handshake, no left-trouser leg, kiss-the-goat type of Mason. More the hairy-chested, gruff-voiced, horny-handed, knock-it-down-and-put-it-up-again, sell-you-a-milestone variety. These are the Cornish stone-masons who come over the mainland every winter to help re-build Tresco. From the left: Peter, Farmer, Tom.

A small island must be self-sufficient in all trades if it is to keep functioning. Unlike the mainland, it is not possible simply to call in an expert to drive over and fix the problem. As a result, many islanders are on call around the clock during the nine-month tourist season. Tresco's visitors pay well to holiday in this beautiful place, and everything has to work for them – without fail. By mid November islanders are ready for a break.

This is the time that most go on holiday. The autumn half-term is an extended holiday for Scilly schools who have a shorter summer holiday than mainland schools since many parents are employed in tourism-related occupations. A survey of Tresco islanders' holiday preferences showed a majority holidayed on other islands – Balearics, Canaries, West Indies etc. Perhaps the salt in the air is hard to give up.

Winter sees another type of visitor. Not tourists, but builders and decorators from Cornwall who arrive to renovate cottages and the hotels or to construct any new building that is needed. It's good employment for them, at a time when work is slack on the mainland, and many return year after year.

Some become real 'winter islanders'. Two such were Tom and Farmer – both stonemasons, and built to lift hundred weights which they frequently did, lugging vast stones into place on walls. I first met them on a boat trip back from St Mary's. Farmer was younger than Tom and introduced him as his father which for a while I accepted at face value. It took some time to realise that both them were masters of the wind-up and loved to practice on islanders whom they considered might be a bit slow or innocent. They were a boisterous breath of fresh air, and often the source of good Cornish jokes.

"In Penzance last week," said Farmer "this car stopped and the driver wound down the window and said to me (imitating a smart accent) 'Can you tell me the best way to Truro?' Are you driving or walking? I asked him. 'Driving, of course' he said. Then that'll be the best way, I said."

Another couple who made a lasting impression were Bob and Barry. They were decorators who every year came to renovate the cottages. They would work hard long into the night, starting early in the morning and got through a huge amount of work cheerfully and efficiently. Soon they became part of the community, helping to organise events while they were here in the winter and joining in all aspects of island life. Within a couple of years they both gave up decorating to become full-time employees on Tresco. Bob took over Gallery Tresco which exhibits Cornish and Scillonian artists and craftsmen,

Barry

while Barry took over Tresco Stores – the island shop – and revitalised it to the extent that it became known as 'Tresco Harrods'.

The pub – the New Inn – was, as one might expect, the social centre of the island. It never bothered to open in those days until about 7.30 pm and no one much got there until about 10 pm. After that, it was a case of 'last one out turns the light off'. I can remember (just) some pretty wild sessions hosted by landlord Chris Hopkins and wife Lesley, who later moved to the neighbouring island of Bryher to open their own pub – Fraggle Rock. Nowadays, the New Inn is managed by the Estate and of course these things never, ever happen!

BEATING FOR THE SHOOT

An important winter activity is the Shoot. This takes place four or five times each winter when Robert and Lucy hosted weekend shooting-parties at the Abbey.

The first I knew about it was when gamekeeper Steve Parkes appeared in the pub recruiting beaters. With memories of Home Counties shoots, and expectations of a gentle ramble over the island I volunteered, showing up at the Farm Shed at 9am on Saturday.

There were canvas leggings for everyone, and a length of Dyno-rod to beat with. Except for me, the team seemed pretty young. I overheard Steve say quietly to several of them: "Keep an eye on the old chap".

On the first drive, Steve lined us up in front of some impenetrable brambles, beyond which lay a wood. Next to me was one of the young gardeners Andrew Lawson, a well-built fitness fanatic. When the whistle blew, Andrew charged into the middle of the thickest brambles like a tank, flailing his arms and grunting. I chose a slightly less dense route but was soon completely ensnared in thorns. I then perfected a technique that was to stand me in good stead for the rest of the day – a sort of swallow-dive followed by a roll. This got me through the first lot of brambles, although I now had blood streaming down my face from scratches, and about ten percent of my clothing had been left in tatters on the bush.

Andrew, as instructed, was waiting as I emerged. I had progressed about ten feet from my starting position. "Alright?" he said. "Great" I replied through the blood "Let's go!"

Andrew Lawson.

Lined up in front of impenetrable brambles.

Andrew continued on his way like a demented combine-harvester, bits of wood and bramble flying in all directions, with an occasional pheasant rising into the air with a squawk of alarm. In the distance ahead of us, we could hear the crack of the guns as the birds that we had put up flew over them.

I continued on my way, swallow-diving and rolling through the undergrowth. Every now and then Steve would blow a whistle and everyone would stop and wait as this extraordinary old man caught up. It probably amused them, and it is greatly to their credit that no one actually burst into audible laughter.

I had hoped that the wood when we finally got there might present easier terrain – and to start with it did. The brambles seemed less developed in the shade. However a new obstacle presented itself. Three massive trees had been up-rooted in a gale and lay rotting in front of us. I clambered up onto the first trunk and fell down between it and the next one. I was unhurt but totally trapped. I could hear the rest of them moving on ahead of me. "Help" I shouted. Then "HELP!!" Then with a mighty crashing in the undergrowth, Andrew appeared. He got me out somehow, and on we went...

When we finished with the wood, we beat through fields, climbed over walls, waded through a swamp, and tramped across endless heather and gorse. We finished near the Abbey at lunchtime, and walked half a mile to the New Inn where a pasty and a pint awaited each of us. It tasted good.

"Now for the really hard part" said Steve encouragingly as we left after lunch. He wasn't joking.

What happened next was like Vietnam. Not that I've been there, but I have seen the films. Walking north of the Hotel, we were positioned in front of a valley full of rhododendrons that had grown to a height of about twenty feet. Someone had cut tunnels through them at intervals. When the whistle blew we each entered a tunnel.

My tunnel was about three and a half feet high, and I crouched double as I walked. After twenty feet it stopped. I was faced by a wall of branches. It was nearly pitch dark in there. Andrew (who else) was with me. Without a word he started climbing upwards, forcing his way through boughs as he went. "I can't believe I'm doing this" I muttered as I followed.

My tunnel was about three and a half feet high.

A valley full of rhododendrons.

Gamekeeper Steve Parkes.

...tramped across endless heather and gorse.

Stuart Brint.

Somehow we forced our way upwards towards the daylight. We were now looking across the tops of the rhododendrons. Andrew started to plunge across this canopy, finding a foothold and lunging onwards, clutching at anything that would keep him up there. He made aerial progress forward, and every now and then a pheasant broke away sailing in the wind towards the guns.

I decided to follow his example, and reverted to my patented swallow-dive-and-roll technique. I made slow progress over the rhodo canopy. Various other beaters had also surfaced, so to speak, and to my absolute amazement, one had dragged a spaniel up there with him. The dog cheerfully forced its way alongside its master in this surreal environment twenty feet above the ground.

All good things must come to an end, and for me it came when I missed a branch in the middle of a swallow-dive and plunged head-first towards the ground. In fact I only fell about four feet before a branch held me, and I lay vertical – head towards the ground. The only way forward now was downwards, and by pulling and wriggling I eventually hit the dirt in the dark at the bottom. Now I could only progress by crawling on my belly through the dirt under branches and hope to find daylight in due course.

Meanwhile, I was surrounded by roars of laughter as one after the other the beaters succumbed to the fate I had suffered and came crashing through the canopy, through the branches, and down to earth. We all ended up crawling in the mud. Finally we emerged into daylight, crawling out at the feet of the guns.

A bit more of this and a lot more tramping over heather and gorse, and it was all over. It had been a good day; the guns had a good bag – pheasant, partridge and woodcock – and we had survived.

I ran a hot bath when I got home, but found that my entire body was scratched so that the hot water stung. But the warmth eased my tired muscles and I slept very deeply that night.

Soccer on Tresco
Like anywhere else, Tresco islanders enjoy soccer – both playing and following their various teams. Unlike the mainland, it can be difficult – the only football pitch on Scilly is on St Mary's, and the nearest Football League team to watch is in Devon.

This has never stopped Tresco islanders from forming soccer teams, and way back before the Second World War there were enough inhabitants for New Grimsby to raise a team to play Old Grimsby.

Several good players have lived on Tresco, including – in my time – more than one who had played semi-professionally on the mainland.

In the early 1990s we would practice on the heliport, before taking a team to St Mary's to play one of the two teams there. We called ourselves the 'OIKs' for 'Off Island Kickers FC' and turned out in a smart yellow and green kit (the colours of Tresco Estate) that was provided by our sponsors – a Devon company called Pot Black Ltd that manufactured pool tables and children's paddling pools.

The games were always fun and a surprisingly high level of football was played. St Mary's could put together a good team if they combined both their island sides and I don't think we ever beat a combined St Mary's team when I was playing. We were able to beat the separate teams though.

We had a good balance of players. Youngsters, mostly gardeners such as

Stuart Brint and Andrew Lawson, who ran well while older more experienced players such as Head Gardener, Mike Nelhams, boatbuilder, Barry Philpott and others – talked a good game and 'let the ball do the work'.

Practice took place on the heliport at the weekends with a five-a-side game. Stuart Brint – the Hotel gardener – had played a bit, but gardener Andrew Lawson hadn't. After Andrew had hacked Stuart down a few times, Stuart complained "You can't do that, Andrew – it's a foul."

"Who says so?" said a puzzled Andrew.

"It's the rules…"

"Bloody silly rules then."

Now, in the new millennium, many young players turn out for the 'OIKs' and most of the old ones have faded away. Scilly remains, however, the most westerly far-flung outpost of England's Beautiful Game.

Our first season against St Mary's was a disaster. We did not win a game against either of their sides. However, the following year the *Tresco Times* was able to report:

OIKs score – sensation!

'Women fainted and brave men went pale when news reached the New Inn that the Off-Island Kickers FC – the OIKS – had not only scored their first ever goal but actually beaten one of the St Mary's teams in a pre-season friendly.

'Like poetry in motion, the OIKs strolled to a 3-1 win against Rovers, having previously lost 0-2 to Rangers. Our lads were over the moon, and are now confident of taking care of the representative St Mary's League team after the humiliation of last season.

'St Mary's has the smallest league in the world (two teams, one pitch) and the

Football teams from the 1950s.

smallest 'gate' – one man who sits in his own portable one-person grandstand. League officials are now confident that it qualifies as an all-seater stadium under the terms of the Taylor Report. Success obviously rubs off; our sponsors Pot Black Limited report record sales of their paddling pools and snooker tables since adopting the OIKs.'

The national newspapers – notably the *Independent* and *The Times* both carried reports on this odd football team from the last piece of England. However, the next *Tresco Times* brought us back to earth.

OIKs talk a good game

The sheer exhilaration of both scoring and winning has been too much for the Off-Island Kickers. They decided to rest on their laurels and not to have a season. No further games were played, many pints were sunk and much talk took place on tactics and what we would do to St Mary's if only the sea wasn't so lumpy and so many players weren't away.

This will be a big disappointment to our readers, and to those of Henry Winter's Sports column in the Independent *to which the Oiks were elevated alongside Liverpool and Arsenal. Yet another case of National Press coverage going to the heads of a promising team, I'm afraid.*

The next edition brought more promising news...

OIKS on International Duty!

Now, the ultimate accolade. The selectors for the Isles of Scilly representative team have chosen two players from the OIKs to play against the Channel islands. Both the Head Gardener and the Heliport Manager will travel. The OIKs' goalkeeper who talks a good game between picking the ball out of the back of the net is staying close to the phone. Just in case they need him.

Few islanders get to see a League game, unless they happen to be on the mainland – up-country – and near a ground at the weekend. Occasionally, though, it was possible to contrive a kind of 'virtual soccer', as this report explained...

Virtual Soccer

Tresco is home to the most westerly English supporters of the following League teams – Portsmouth, Reading, Exeter and (inevitably) Manchester United and Liverpool. It's seldom that the fans get a chance to see their heroes, so it was a great day when a Sunday match between Reading and Portsmouth was televised live... except that West Country, our local ITV franchise declined to show it.

However, a home-based Reading fan agreed to record the broadcast, and sent down the tape with the match programme. The game was then replayed a few days later at the home of our local Reading supporter.

The Pompey fan took up his position in the armchair reserved for away supporters, and battle commenced with appropriate insults ("You're not singing anymore!") as the game unfolded.

Half-time was observed in the most realistic way possible – standing in the garden in the rain with a cup of Bovril and a glutinous meat pie.

At the end of the game, the Pompey supporter trudged home across the island – no trouble leaving the ground – to a sympathetic wife ("Good game, dear? Who won?"). It came close to the real thing... it really did

Insular Things 2

GREAT RESULT FOR THE FISH! Spring 1997

The wreck the next day – Flemart is an anagram of Ram Left.

It is estimated that there are 521 shipwrecks around Scilly. On 15 August, the 522nd occurred at 4am when a Newlyn fishing vessel left St Mary's harbour and collided with Crow Rock – a substantial, well-marked local feature.

This is the maritime equivalent of colliding with a lamp-post in the desert. The fishing boat *Flemart* [anagram of Ram Left? Ed] sprang a leak, was abandoned – then sank near Crow Bar. The three crew were rescued by the lifeboat, one sustaining a broken jaw, one a broken arm, and the third a nasty shock on his first trip to sea.

Other fishermen who had been ashore with them until 3.30am expressed amazement at how the accident could possibly have happened.

Meanwhile the fish in the vessel's hold swam away – presumably thinking "Thank you God. It's a miracle, a miracle!" – thus stirring surreal speculation about the Meaning of Life.

Agapanther

Islanders cannot keep dogs on the island, so the alternative for many people is a cat. We took on a monster tabby tom from someone who was leaving the island. Tigger was the son of a feral cat and a domestic moggy from St Martin's and fathered many of the island cat population. When he died of kidney failure, we were devastated and decided to find a replacement.

After perusing the small ads in *Cat World*, I called a man who advertised 'Big Cats for Sale'. He lived in Milton Keynes.

"I would like a large cat, please."

"How big do you want it guv?"

"Well... large. How big do they come?"

Agapanther.

"Oh, larger than a terrier. They're lovely, guv. A cross between a Snow Leopard and an Occicat."

"Are you sure I don't need a licence? I only want a large cat, not a Big Cat."

"You'll be fine, guv. I've sold scores of them."

"Are they fierce?"

"Nah. Docile, guv. Lovely temperament. Mind you, they can look after themselves if they have to... they don't go looking for trouble though."

"How much are they?"

"Two thousand pound each, guv."

"WHAT! I only want a moggy..."

"Oh, <u>pet-quality</u>... You should have said, guv. Thought you wanted one for breeding. I can let you have pet-quality for a hundred."

And so we bought Agapanther, the most beautiful but savage cat in the world. Within a few months he'd trashed half the cats on the island, and cost a fortune in vet's bills to sew them back together.

It also became apparent that he couldn't stomach tinned pet food preferring his meals warm and bloody – rabbits, rats and, I fear, pheasant. Sadly, we realized that Agapanther had reverted to his ancestral state. A beautiful but wild thing.

He disappeared shortly afterwards, never to be seen again.

Giant agave in New Grimsby.

AGAVE ATQUE VALE

Tresco's Triffid – an agave that grew to 45 feet in a year – was finally laid to rest (i.e. chopped down) this October after blocking Daphne Jenkins' view for the summer. Its seeds may flower again in about 50 years' time. It made headlines in the National Press – as did a Yucca, its cousin, which grew 14 feet in 2 weeks in 1977 on Tresco – thus becoming the fastest growing plant in the world, (viz. *The Guinness Book of Records*).

GUMMER BARES HIS TEETH   Spring 1994

In the last edition of the *Tresco Times* we were far from pleased with Prime Minister, John Major, after he stated that British beaches were in an acceptable state – despite various court cases pending from people who appear actually to have been poisoned after swimming off the English mainland.

Now Environment Minister, Mr John Gummer, has criticised European bureaucrats because they black-flagged these polluted places. This really is not good enough. For once the Europeans are right.

So clean up your act – we think your attitude sucks, Mr Gummer. *The Tresco Times* expects to see action from you to stop this mainland pollution scandal – and no more of this silly nonsense.

THE TRESCO TIMES CRITIC REVIEWS THE ONLY FILM-SHOW ON TRESCO

What a pleasure to be able to report on a film that is suitable for all members of the family. *Helicopter Passenger Safety* (U) is British International

Helicopters' first film. It is now playing to full houses up to 20 times a day in selected venues in Penzance and on Scilly.

I caught the movie on Tresco in Terminal One at the heliport. The plot is a challenging one – and works on several levels. At its most basic, it is a simple what-if idea. What if – "in the unlikely event" – something should go wrong on a routine helicopter flight?

The passengers are beautifully cast, and turn in surreal performances as the kind of wooden dummies one hopes never to have to share a flight with. Watch as the pretty girl slowly and carefully straps herself in. Who is the mysterious bearded man who appears in every scene? What is the director telling us? The tension builds, we suspect that there will be an emergency..... and yes, soon the attractive stewardess is in the aisle putting on a life-jacket. She smiles, we see someone else deliberately take out a life-jacket from under the seat... and then a man carefully and slowly unhooks a safety tag and pushes out a window! He leans out before the director freezes the action. What is happening...? Has he been sick, is he escaping? We never know.

The sly humour in the advice not to erect umbrellas when boarding always gets a laugh – although it doesn't reach the heights of farce achieved by the rival Skybus production (not shown on Tresco) which comically reassures us that "it is not necessary to wear your lifejacket in the aircraft".

An alien twist
On a deeper level, the director provides a roller-coaster ride of emotions. The audience on Tresco laughed dryly at the beginning of the movie when the narrator cynically tells them that they will soon be flying to the Isles of Scilly. This aptly reflects the impossible dream of always travelling towards your holidays and never going back to reality.

The drama of the "emergency" during which no passenger shows any sign of panic or concern, and the mildly erotic moment as the winsome stewardess inflates her life-jacket are all cleverly played. It soon dawns on the audience that (of course!) all the blandly smiling passengers and crew must be aliens – or on Prozac. What sort of trip are they all about to take? The brilliantly dead-pan script and the Pearl & Dean music on the soundtrack both underline the director's point – we're all space cadets.

Better than the play
Visitors who have been coming for years to the islands will wonder whether this film is as good as the stage-show on which it is based – which used to be performed live in the helicopter before every take-off. I have to say that it is, and that it pushes the boundaries of film-making to new frontiers. It's good value too. Ten minutes of entertainment seems like hours.

This surreal film is quite suitable for a family audience, and must by now have achieved cult status among film buffs. It may even give Disney pause for thought. I happily recommend it as an excellent and highly amusing way to start and finish your holiday.

Helicopter Passenger Safety U Cert
Also showing in Penzance

MAJOR APPOINTMENT
It used to be said that you could walk into any village pub and ask "Major been in?" and get a sensible response. Not on Tresco... until now. A Major has

Major Bryan Wright.

therefore been imported – Bryan Wright. Bryan is an eccentric who has travelled the world before coming to rest here as our Official Guide. He is very familiar with Tresco, is related to Mr Dorrien Smith and is a fund of amusing anecdotes. For a modest fee you can enjoy a gentlemanly and educated stroll with him – or attend one of his weekly evening slide shows at the Hotel. He's also always up for a game of bridge.

Snow sometimes comes to Scilly. This Christmas Card scene is a rare example of sub-tropical snow on Tresco.

Roger Oyler marries Ann.

Roger's parents marry.

Roger and Ann's daughter Fran marries Stuart Brint.

Finally here are pictures of three generations of an island family getting married.

CHAPTER TWENTY ONE

island race   *proud of it...*

A Waffle with "The Commodore"

Some time around late March or early April, there's a subtle change in the wind. Suddenly one can sniff summer round the corner.

The sea that looked threatening most days in the winter now takes on a benign look for several days running. This is when I walk round to the field where the *Waffler* has spent her hibernation.

Henry, the Harbourmaster, has all the Estate boats to prepare, and this is when I start my negotiations with him to let me put the *Waffler* under cover in his boat shed so that I can rub her down, and paint her with a new coat of Britannia Blue gloss, some red anti-fouling and Swedish wood oil on her wood-work. Usually by mid-May I have her ready.

It's a good discipline to prepare your own boat. I know every screw, rivet, block, cleat. Just to be sure I usually ask the professionals at Bryher boatyard to cast an eye over her. After all, when sailing alone out of sight behind Round Island, say, the last thing you want is a gear failure.

The *Celtic Waffler* was a gift from Robert and Lucy. One Christmas over a drink, Lucy gave me a present. It was about three foot long by six inches wide and wrapped prettily in Christmas wrapping. I opened it to find a hand-painted name board – *CELTIC WAFFLER* it read. I laughed, thinking it a happy joke on my verbosity.

'Let me show you where it goes' said Lucy, and led me around the corner. There, on a trailer, sat a Cornish Coble – once part of the Estate's boat-hire fleet, and now painted up by Henry, gleaming in the sunlight.....

It was probably the most thoughtful and enjoyable present that I have ever received.

I do not believe that there is anywhere else in Europe where you can have as much fun in small sailing boats. Scilly has everything – uninhabited islands, impressive rocks, white sand beaches, clear blue sea, big tides, an abundance of sea-birds and seals – and the occasional porpoise or dolphin if you're lucky.

Amazingly, the waters here are almost free of other craft. Larger yachts tend to stay put on their moorings once they get here, or only venture into the

The Celtic Waffler.

main channels. This leaves the narrows and shallows, and some awesome rocks, to us small fry and the local boatmen. It's a select club. An experienced yachtsman – now a regular visitor with his daysailer – says: "I sail past reefs with the waves breaking over them, through tiny channels between rocks... things that would have scared me silly a few years ago".

Even if you're a landlubber you can probably imagine the fun of taking an open boat around the North End in a running sea, or nosing through the rocks in a light summer's breeze, chart in hand ("I think we can make it, it's half-tide and there should be just enough water. Shout if you see anything and be ready to raise the centre-board").

BOY'S OWN VOYAGES

These are times when middle-aged men become teenagers again, and every voyage becomes a Boy's Own adventure. Perhaps you have to be middle-aged to appreciate losing twenty or thirty years for an hour or two. Those of us brought up in the Ian Proctor school of dinghy sailing (circa late-1950s) know that the correct rig afloat is a sweater and a pair of shorts... two pairs of shorts in winter. Life jackets are of course de rigeur for everyone afloat, but I am not sure about the expensive yellow off-shore foul-weather designer gear. Clumsy to write, clumsy to wear. Looks good in the pub though.

AUTUMN EVENINGS

Spring and early summer is usually idyllic and so is September and parts of October. Quite often it is the two extreme ends of the season that provide some of the most memorable days on the water.

I remember a calm September evening after a warm afternoon spent on Samson. Reluctant to use the outboard, we were slowly coming home on the tide to New Grimsby. Suddenly we realised that – for a magic moment – the sunset had painted everything a rose-coloured pink. We floated, suspended in a rose-pink world.... the land, the sea, ourselves, and – so it seemed – the very air we breathed.

Only a few days later, on the other side of the island we had watched the sun go down over Borough Farm as we came up-channel to Old Grimsby, running before a gentle breeze. In the after-light of the sunset, with a partial cloud covering, the colours of Tresco were replaced by a gentle silver light that danced off the sea and filtered everything with a metallic silver sheen... as beautiful and subtle as anything we had seen before.

A HAPPY DISCOVERY AND A NASTY SURPRISE

This was the year that I "discovered" Forman's Island – a tiny islet off Old Grimsby where a white sand beach lies exposed between low-water and half-tide and is perfectly positioned to view a summer sunset with a glass of chilled Chablis to hand. There are enough surprises to be discovered in a boat on Scilly to last a lifetime or two.

Some are not always pleasant. A late October storm – suddenly Force 10 and blowing from the East – came howling into the normally sheltered Old Grimsby harbour. It stayed for a long night, while my Cornish Coble that had carried me through the summer bucked and pulled at her mooring like a teth-ered horse in a stable fire.

In the morning, the mooring lug on the Coble had sheared, releasing the bob-stay, collapsing the rigging and bringing down the mast – but she had stayed safe, secured by a safety strop to her mooring, although with half the rigging over the side. When I got to her at low water, the strop was half-worn through after just three hours of chafing the fairleads.

AN ISLAND SOLUTION

How do you recover a damaged daysailer on a beach in a Force 10? Easily, if it's on Tresco. Within quarter of an hour Nick Shiles arrived in the JCB, Harbourmaster Henry Birch followed on a flat-bed trailer behind a tractor driven by brother Eddie. Webbing strops were placed fore and aft under the hull, and attached to the teeth of the JCB bucket. The Coble was swung up and gently placed on the flat-bed. Total time spent on the beach... under five minutes. After close inspection, the Coble was little the worse for wear – and the mooring lug will be replaced with a heavy-duty version. Next time I will remember to raise the extra safety stay which would have kept the rigging secure when the bob-stay broke.

BIRD NOTES BY DAVID ROSAIR

'To date almost 150 species of birds have been observed over the months of April, May, June, September and October. Apart from all the common species of migrants many unusual species have been recorded.

'Spring highlights over the last 10 years include a superb Hoopoe feeding in the open grass on Vane Hill in early morning sunlight, whilst a Golden Oriole flighting in off the sea across Great Porth thrilled everyone in the group. A Red-rumped Swallow hawking over the Great Pool proved to be a new species for most of the participants, a Woodchat Shrike above Gimble Porth was observed before breakfast, whilst a Sardinian Warbler behind the Quayside Cafe in full song was definitely the bird of the Tour for many!

'Autumn traditionally produces rare birds from both America and Asia and a decade of observations have given pleasure to hundreds of participants. Solitary, Semi-palmated and White-rumped Sandpipers, along with Lesser Yellowlegs have all been observed around the muddy fringes of the Great Pool, a Yellow-rumped

Lapwing.

Warbler along the Middle Fields, Red-breasted Flycatcher and Yellow-browed Warblers at Borough Farm and a splendid Rock Thrush above Hell Bay, Bryher are just some of the ornithological highlights that immediately come to mind.

'Of course there have been changes over the last 10 years, with time standing still for no man. All three hotels have been or are undergoing modification and refurbishment to the benefit of all visitors, while weather patterns are slowly altering which has resulted in subtle population changes within the ornithological world.

'Some things never change – like the sheer peace and tranquility of the islands, the autumn sunrise over the Eastern Isles, the early morning beauty of the Great Pool, the magic of looking out to Mincarlo at dusk... to name a few!

'Very early this May morning I walked around Gimble Perth and over Castledown to Cromwell's Castle. The weather vane above the Island Hotel entrance showed a very slight northerly breeze and the brilliant morning light reflected beautifully from the water between Tresco and St Martins.

'In the spaces of just thirty minutes a Wheatear landed on the roof of the Hotel, Kittiwakes called on the nesting grounds, three Oystercatchers "kleeped" over the bay in flight, both Willow Warbler and Whitethroat sang from the bushes, a Raven alighted no more than 50 metres in front of me and Guillemots whizzed low over the deep blue water to their nesting grounds on Men a Vaur. As I strolled back to the Island Hotel for breakfast I again realised how privileged I was to be once again leading a Birdwatching Tour on the most beautiful archipelago in the world, an experience never to be taken for granted.

'Some things never change!'

CHAPTER TWENTY TWO
CRICKET IN THE SUMMER

When you arrive on Tresco and disembark from the helicopter, you are standing usually at about deep mid-off. Tresco Heliport is also Tresco Cricket Ground. For this reason, games are played on Sundays when no helicopters land. The wicket is a rubberised material laid over concrete; in fact, a perfect batting track that gives nothing to a bowler.

Cricket at the Heliport.

Tresco cricketers are a mixed bag, like many village teams. A few will have played to some sort of reasonable club level, and at least one was a former Minor County player. But for the most part, Tresco cricketers are enthusiastic but untutored players with a good eye. This is as it should be, because in a 25-over-per-side game there's no time for finesse, and with temptingly short boundaries on island grounds, sixes and fours abound. It's entertaining stuff, and always played in a friendly atmosphere. Sportsmanship is still valued on Scilly.

Visitors enjoy watching the games, which are accompanied by home-made teas served by Ann Oyler. Several visitors have even joined the team when Tresco was short of players. Two distinguished visitors, Nick Treadaway the former Sussex fast bowler and Bill Lake the England Youth Coach have both taken time out of their holidays to coach the team in the basics of the game.

A few players deserve special mention, not least Lewis 'Morse' Gaillard. Morse, as he became known to everyone, was in his early twenties when he was hired as a Kitchen Porter in the Island Hotel.

"What's your name, boy?" asked the Chef

"Lewis Gaillard."

"I can't remember that," snorted the Chef. "Lewis, eh? Well from now on I'll call you Morse." The name stuck.

Morse had two passions. One was the rock group Queen and an obsession with lead singer Freddie Mercury, the other was cricket. He grew a moustache and tried to look like Freddie Mercury, and he bought the complete replica kit of Somerset Cricket Club. When he turned out for Tresco, he became Ian Botham.

Morse played every game as if it was a Lords Test Match. When he walked out to bat in his whites, his Somerset shirt and helmet, the sand-dunes and hummocks of Tresco faded away to be replaced by the Lords pavilion and the green sward of the most famous ground in the world. The opposition were never St Agnes or St Martin's, they were always Australia or the West Indies.

Morse was not a bad player, but a tendency to imagine that he *was* Botham and then to play *his* favourite shot – a stylish but risky sweep – meant that he never scored as many runs as he might have done. He was also a fast but erratic bowler.

Morse did, however, achieve something that very few cricketers enjoy – temporary national fame. The BBC Radio's Test Match Special debated Morse's unique bowling figures in a match for Tresco. It was during a rain break at Lords, and for ten minutes Henry Blofeld and the other commentators discussed the saga of Morse, and the most remarkable bowling figures ever recorded. This is the report that they had spotted in the *Tresco Times*:

CRICKET AT THE HELIPORT   Spring 1994

In our last edition we described Tresco's excellent season of 1993 – a clean sweep of victories against the other off-islands.

*The most extraordinary performance of the season was Lewis "Morse" Gaillard's figures in one match of 5 overs, no maidens, 3 wickets for 14 runs **OF WHICH 10 WERE WIDES**. This probably rates a mention in Wisden, and will no doubt puzzle cricket historians forever.*

Fast bowler Morse's first ball struck gully sharply and painfully on the knee, and he then proceeded to spray various close fielders as far away as short-square-leg with quick balls on a good length. None were anywhere near the astonished batsman.

After some discussion with his perplexed captain it became clear that Morse was not his usual self. The previous night he had been concussed after colliding with an unlit bicycle following a few drinks in the pub. He had then discharged himself from hospital in order to play in the match.

It took a bit of trial and error (and a few more wides) to establish which of the three batsmen that Morse could see was "real" – but once things were clear the wickets fell, and Morse retired with bowling figures that will probably never be repeated as long as the game is played.

Having made national radio and being written up in the national press, Morse left Tresco, and was last heard of working in a 'Little Chef' in Cornwall. From another cricket report in the *Tresco Times* of the same year, we come across another milestone:

Maiden Bowled Billy Over

We must mention carpenter Billy Pritchard's outstanding contribution to Tresco Cricket Club lore. In a recent match against Truro Doctors the opposition included two women players. Billy did his stuff nobly for Women's Lib by becoming the first Tresco player ever to be caught by one female off the bowling of another.

But soon another Tresco player was in the national papers, and even managed to be made 'Fielder of the Year' by Simon Barnes' New Year column in the *Times*. Once again, the *Tresco Times* printed the story first:

TRESCO SIGNS OVERSEAS PLAYER

Our last report on Tresco cricket – describing Morse's argument with an unlit bicycle and his subsequent bowling spell – received wide media attention. Unfortunately, he appears not to listen to Radio 3 or to take the quality broadsheets. He is still missing – somewhere on the mainland. This has left a gap in the team that the Club has filled – occasionally with visitors – and now with an overseas player.

Not for us someone as obvious as a West Indian or an Australian – Tresco does things differently. We have recruited Cakra from Bali. This is a country where cricket does not seem to be played. At any rate, Cakra has never seen it played. He is here to work as a cottage cleaner during the season and sportingly stepped into Morse's shoes.

Billy Pritchard

And what a worthy replacement he is. After only ten minutes instruction on the laws of the game, he took his place at extra cover having been told to shy the ball in to the wicket-keeper if it came his way, and to catch it if possible. An hour later, he had held two fine catches, had run out a batsman and severely bruised the wicket-keeper's hands several times an over.

It seems that his athleticism stems from a love of table tennis, and considerable experiece in vermin control in his native land. This took the form of slinging stones at squirrels (well, they are tree-rats) and other small furry mammals. After watching the Tresco bowling attack, Cakra reckoned he could do better and delivered a few balls which surprised everyone but which were sadly counted as illegal – at least until they change the laws. His technique was to rush to the wicket and deliver a fast and unplayable baseball pitch just short of a length. So far, he has yet to bat.

In the meantime, captain and Gamekeeper Steve Parkes reckons he may be able to offer Cakra some overtime – helping keep down the island rat population.

Playing away on St Agnes or St Martin's is always fun, since it involves a boat trip and plenty to drink. The highlight of the season is the Triangle Match played between Tresco, St Martin's and St Agnes. Each team plays each other over the course of a day – three matches, hence the name.

In 1994 Tresco travelled to St Agnes as champions. But then it started to go wrong...

TRESCO SHIPWRECKED   Winter 1994

'It's a funny old game, cricket.

'Last year Tresco were Champions of the Test Series between ourselves, St Martin's and St Agnes, and winners of the Triangle Match. This year we couldn't get arrested.

'Perhaps the Triangle Match, played this year on St Agnes, summed up our season. The day started happily enough as Firethorn *took us on the "scenic" route to St Agnes passing baby seals, birds and a basking Sunfish. St Agnes was reached as a fine drizzle started.*

'Our first game was lost closely to St Martin's – Mike Pender needing only one run off the last ball to tie. He gambled on glory and the big hit to win the game – and was bowled. One down. The second match – against St Agnes – saw us needing a win to share the spoils.

'Batting second we simply ran out of time to make the score, and St Agnes deservedly took the trophy for the first time ever. Many congratulations to them – the smallest of the off-islands.

'Splendid food after the game was followed by some cheerful carousing in the Turk's Head, until we took to the boats for the return trip in the dark. Some made it, one didn't. A rapidly ebbing tide, and shifting sands left half the team and your correspondent stranded – firmly aground in the Bryher Channel.

'Despite cheerful cries of "it's OK, we can walk from here", we were rescued by a local in a rowing boat and left at Appletree Bay, where we stumbled ashore under the stars like a damp and defeated army.

'Trekking home we found the New Inn about to close. Our favourite Scilly bar-steward Robin was persuaded to administer liquid first-aid before we finally made it back to our beds. Ah well, there's always next year...'

Robin Lawson

CHAPTER TWENTY THREE

island race   *proud of it...*   # A Waffle with "The Commodore"

Sometimes in the summer the weather can just be too fine. Too gentle for sailing with no breeze at all on the water...

One of the best sounds in the world is the chuckle of water around the hull as a sailing-boat picks up speed under a light wind. So too is the creak of timber as the *Celtic Waffler* heels away under a stiff breeze.

After an early summer of variable weather, came glorious August with hot sun, blue skies and light breezes. Too light for sailing at times...

When the wind dies to nothing, and the August sun beats down from an azure sky, those of us who enjoy sailing are forced to fall back on outboard engines. I suppose that the more energetic would say what's wrong with rowing, but when you get to my age....

So it was, one hot still afternoon that we set out – my companion and I – in the *Celtic Waffler* with the 4-horse Yamaha chuntering on the transom. Gone were the gentle sounds of sail, we'd become a "stink-pot". For some people the world of power-boating consists of rushing up and down as fast as possible, with or without a skier in tow. We felt that there might be fun in challenging Neptune more demandingly and less noisily.

The vast, brooding bulk of Men a Vaur off the north of St Helen's seemed a good place to start. The two enormous cathedral-sized rocks are separated by a narrow channel at high-water. It's wide enough for a boat like the Coble, but an underwater boulder half-way into the channel is a reminder not to choose a day with any significant swell.

Men a Vaur.

Round Island.

INTO THE UNDERWORLD

We went through with enough speed to maintain steerage way, but not enough to create a displacement that would suck us onto one wall or the other. Above us the sheer dark rock rose vertically to a tiny slit of the sky. The dampness and cold contrasted with the warmth we had just left outside. We thought of the thousands of tons of water that is thrown through here in a second during a winter storm. We were trespassing in the lair of a mighty and unforgiving God. We came out the other side buoyed up by our bravery – turned round, and went through the other way thumbing our noses... tiny, insignificant beings in Neptune's Netherworld.

Then off round the North End where The Kettle simmered gently even in this calm sea – tons of water climbing a few feet up the rocks and slopping down again. All around it the surface of the sea lifted and fell. Next, we were looking at Shipman's Head at the end of Bryher. A tall-cliffed rocky island in its own right – separated from the main island by a narrow channel only just wider than the Coble. But this was a quite different scene to Men a Vaur. Two local teenagers, tanned by the sun, laughed and shouted as they jumped from the low cliffs into the sunny water before climbing out and doing it all over again. A scene from some Greek Idyll. We passed through as they waved to us – just about a foot to spare on each side.

So we found our way to Hell Bay, rock-hopping through channels and seaweed, then past Samson, and a short motor across to White Island. We decided to land and – in a flat calm sea, remember – I leapt out with difficulty onto the rocky beach. My companion reversed out while I explored the island where the survivors of the *Delaware* had been rescued. It's hard to exaggerate the level of seamanship that the pilots of Bryher must have exhibited that December day in 1871. Regaining the Coble with some difficulty, we made off to Scilly Rock – the huge mass of rock which almost rivals Men a Vaur. It was here that the *Isabo* came to grief in 1927 and where again the men of Bryher and St Mary's distinguished themselves in another remarkable rescue.

Scilly Rock is another place with an awesome appearance – and a narrow channel through the middle. At each end, are reefs just below the surface. We could see lobster-pot buoys in amongst them, so someone knew how to get in close...

We circled around, tried to make up our mind – in the end deciding to give Neptune best. Enough for one day, and back to Old Grimsby for a sundowner! In the balmy warmth of evening we ended up sitting on the wooden deck behind the cottage.

The Editor joined us for a glass or two as we watched the evening sun sink low enough in the sky to cut through a gap in the hedge that shelters the garden from the field beyond. For a moment the leaves were back-lit and luminous against the dark shadows of the hedge – and the last rays picked out the blue tips of the lavender. "It seldom gets much better than this" said the Editor – as he uncorked another bottle of chilled Chablis.

A few days later the wind was up to an easy Force 3 so we sailed to the Eastern Isles, landing on Nour Nour. This tiny island is my favourite of all. A sandy beach is exposed at three-quarter tide, the seals swim in the channel between you and Great Ganilly, and you can sit and eat your picnic among the best-preserved pre-Roman remains on Scilly.

"Why is it?" asked the Editor, who was chewing his Bryher crab sandwich "that no one eats hot lobster any more? I have a friend in Long Island who cooks his lobsters for exactly eight minutes in boiling water and serves them piping-hot. He covers the table with newspapers, invites his friends to wear their oldest clothes, provides each with a hammer, pliers and pointy skewer – and everyone gets to work. Break your lobster open down the spine, take out the meat and dip it in melted butter and Cayenne pepper. Best accompanied with freshly-fried chips, green salad and ice-cold champagne or Tours de Gendres. A messy business alright, but quite delicious!"

"And the newspapers?" I asked.

"Scoop up the debris in the newspapers... Simple and effective way to clear the table."

We agreed that cold lobster was a bad second to the hot version – and that fresh-cooked crab might be better than both.

"Another good sound," said the Editor, smiling happily as he lay on the soft peat among the sea-pinks "is the squeak, pop, glug-glug as the cork is drawn and the cold wine poured. The dew quickly forming on the glass.... then the sharp crack as you break open the first lobster..." He stretched contentedly "They're all happy sounds of summer – like that chuckle of water round the hull of the *Celtic Waffler* – and they will always remind me of Scilly."

I had to agree with my friend. "We are," I said "among the luckiest of men."

CHAPTER TWENTY FOUR

THE BOYS OF '66 AND AN OIK

I t was an idyllic evening in the summer and I had decided to go sailing. I was preparing the boat on the beach in Old Grimsby when I heard a voice call my name. It belonged to an old friend – a banker – who was staying in the Island Hotel. Eddy Charlton ran a bank and I suppose was down for a bit of relaxation.

"That looks fun," he said "can I come?"

So I took Eddy sailing. He had never been in a sailing boat before, and we sailed gently round St Helen's Pool and Tean, enjoying a cold glass or two of white wine. "I can see why people get hooked on sailing," said Eddy. Then... "The bank has sponsored a boat in the Fastnet race next month, perhaps I'll join the crew." I tried to explain that there would be a big difference between my little boat and the high tech, stripped-out racing machine that tries to win the Fastnet.

A couple of months later, Eddie called me from London. "I want to thank you" he said "for introducing me to sailing. I joined the crew and we won the Fastnet."

Well, I suppose that that was the fastest sailing career ever.

I had played soccer with Eddie years before, for an Old Boy team, and then later for a veterans' soccer team that we called the OAFs – the Old Age Footballers. I had heard that Eddie's bank was due to sponsor a reunion dinner for the World Cup soccer team of 1966. In return for introducing him to sailing, I begged a ticket.

Meeting the heroes of '66 was a thrill, and I wrote it up for the *Tresco Times*. Danny Baker of *The Times* thought it was pretty funny, and the result was his even-funnier half page in the Saturday Sport section, which is reprinted below:

By Danny Baker

THE TOUCHING STORY OF HOW A MAN FINALLY TRUMPED HIS BROTHER'S WORLD CUP GLORY

Joey Bishop, probably the least celebrated member of the legendary Las Vegas Rat Pack, once summed up Frank Sinatra by saying: "Frank's the kind of guy who, when he gets to heaven, will give God a hard time for making him bald."

A terrific line to be sure and there can be few of us who, upon hearing it, don't take a heretical moment to reflect just what part of our lives we might choose to nitpick about while otherwise glorying in the serene presence of Our Lord. For example, I have a friend who feels his slight stammer stopped him being the greatest stand-up comedian since Arthur English. Another believes that his innate and extraordinary love of draught Guinness has cruelly robbed him of the chance to be very slim and therefore, he-insists, fantastically handsome.

His wife interprets this as a slight upon her, suspecting he regrets that this boozy fetish has denied him a shot at Jennifer Anniston, thus causing him to "settle" for her. So, in return, she reminded him that if she had a better chin she would have been off with Mel Gibson years ago.

You can see what a bombshell of a party game this is. However, every so often one comes across a story where it appears God has had some kind of Almighty pang of conscience and has taken time to correct the blight previously visited upon some poor wretch. Such a story concerns Mr Richard Barber, who initially contacts me under the belief that there may be some sort of cash prize on offer to whoever can claim to be the most westerly British reader of this column. If there were such a competition, Mr Barber would be our winner residing as he does on Tresco, one of the tiny 'off-islands' beyond the central Scillies.

Mention of the Scillies will fire up the imagination of all football fans because it is here we can find St Mary's, home of the smallest soccer league m the world. St Mary's famously has just two teams and one pitch and is featured as a "colour piece" by On The Ball about once-a fortnight.

However Mr Barber's letter alerts us to an even more peculiar set-up on Tresco, where there is just one team and no pitch whatsoever. This wandering squad are called The Off Island Kickers, or Oiks. Richard was once their goalkeeper and, if I catch his drift correctly, they exist purely as some kind of palate-cleansing sorbet side who take on one of the two St Mary's outfits whenever those teams grow sick of the sight of each other.

Now then. Mr Barber has an elder brother, Charles. In July 1966, in the hours after England's World Cup victory, Charles and his chum Alec Foster decided to act where most of the nation were happy simply to celebrate. Rather than merely link arms and dance in the street with the neighbours, Mr Barber Snr realized that there was only one party in town worth attending and that party was being thrown at the Royal Garden Hotel where the England players themselves were actually in attendance.

Donning their fanciest waistcoats, both he and Foster piled into a Mini and drove it across London straight into the basement car park of the relevant Kensington hotspot. Completely unchallenged, they then walked into a service elevator and moments after pushing the button dearly marked "reception suites" found themselves in animated conversation with both George Cohen and Harold Wilson about what an absolutely terrific day it had been.

The OIKs – the Off Island Kickers FC, 1993.

Allegedly, in the next day's front-page photographs of the England team waving out on the hotel balcony that night, there are two unfamiliar faces to be seen beaming through the large windows behind them. These, we can now reveal, are Charles Barber and Alec Foster, gatecrashers.

We naturally, no younger brother can grow up in the shadow of such a sporting story without feeling that God had especially and cruelly marked him out for a lifetime walking in the family doldrums. At gatherings, Richard would sit and smoulder as all the women adoringly clustered around Charles begging for one more telling of The World Cup Story. At even the gayest and most sumptuous weddings, it would take only the slightest reference to Geoff Hurst or Martin Peters before, as Wilde put it, "all was bitter herbs and funeral baked meats".

Little wonder, then, that this particular branch of the Barber family tree soon made his home on the farthest-flung speck of a nation whose greatest sporting triumph was his own personal torment. Worse still, in the fortunes of England's ensuing World Cup campaigns, the likelihood that Richard would ever assuage the sorrow in his soul by gatecrashing an ultimate victory party of his own shrank into distant nothingness.

He would always be Richard-who-never-went, the Richard-who-stayed... and became King John.

Now let us come forward over three long and empty decades to a meeting of old schoolfriends in London. Richard is among their number and so is one Edward "no relation" Charlton, who has risen to become a managing director of Banque Internationale á Luxembourg. The bank, as I hardly need tell you, is part of the Franco-Belgian Dexia group and this miraculous conglomerate, it turns out, is looking for ways to strengthen its profile through sporting ties.

Edward mentions, almost absent-mindedly, that the group is, for instance, about to sponsor a lunch to honour The Boys Of '66. Well can you imagine? As the conversation continues, Richard stands dumbstruck, the room doing a watusi around him, all sound being fed through a phaser like, if you will, the middle bit of Itchycoo Park.

At an appropriate and decent break, Richard finds the composure to sidle up to Edward, who he now realises more than ever is a thoroughly splendid chap and as old and dear a chum as a man can have. Within moments, an invitation to the looming exclusive nose-bag at the Grosvenor House Hotel is extended his way and an end to the hurt in the Barber heart is perhaps in sight.

Ten days later there is Cohen and Ball and Jack and Bobby and all other surviving members of the squad and there also, even if he has not quite the courage actually to strike up a conversation, in the same room is Richard. Nevertheless, he realises that some kind of proof-of-presence will be needed if he is to physically lay the ghost of his brother's domination within the family and, for the first time since they were lads, look him in the eye man to man.

What to do? An autograph? No, this was a banking community business lunch at the Grosvenor House, not the stage door of a Smash Hits poll winners' concert. A jokey photograph with Nobby Stiles perhaps, cheerily passed off as a necessary embarrassing request from a young nephew? Better, except this would necessitate a camera of some sort and Richard did not have one.

Just as he begins toying with the idea of some wet cement and a set of hand-prints, the England players are called into a group for an official photo to hang in the bank's London boardroom. It is now as they gather in one place that Richard notices that, in fact, all are not present. Gordon Banks has had to make his excuses.

From somewhere, and Richard still is at a loss to explain quite from where his actions sprang, in the seconds of silence just as the Boys Of '66 are about to say "cheese", he spoke out. "You're missing a keeper," he calls from the back of his group, then seizing the moment of attention, goes for goal. "I've stood between the posts in my time you know..."

As the laughter pealed out, famous buttocks shift along their chairs and room is made, centre stage, among the legendary line-up, for the disbelieving and long-suffering former goalkeeper of the Oiks – the team from a place with no pitch.

Flash! The second is captured and Richard Barber instantly feels a tremendous weight lift and a lifelong shadow pass from him. Not for him some barely discernible face gatecrashing in the gloom of a balcony window, an image that, incidentally, wasn't even carried in most later editions. Here in the full glory of light, colour and perfect composition are, to all intents and purposes, the existing members of the team that beat the world on July 30, 1966. Thank you, God.

Back row: *Wilf McGuiness (coach), Kenneth Wolstenholme, George Cohen, Nobby Stiles, Roger Hunt, Alan Ball.* Front row: *Martin Peters, Jack Charlton, an OIK, Sir Bobby Charlton, Sir Geoff Hurst.*

Thirty-four years of hurt are ended and the Barbers can be a family once again, although as Richard closes his letter he trusts the Lord will overlook just a little swanking over the Christmas dinner table this year...

(© Danny Baker/*The Times*, 6 January 2001.)

CHAPTER TWENTY FIVE

island race   *proud of it...*

A Waffle with "The Commodore"

Ghosts, Druids... and Joseph of Arimathea?

When the Sou' Wester comes storming into Tresco after raging across three thousand miles of wet ocean – the wind howling round the window frames and the rain cracks against the panes – then all a man wants is a comfortable chair, the clink of ice in a glass of Malt, and an old friend with whom to spin some improbable yarns.

So it was, one late Spring day, that I settled back in the leather arm-chair, kicked a log into life on the fire, and fell to conjecturing about some much earlier Cornish residents with my old friend The Editor...

It was the subject of Ghosts that got us started. There are a couple of haunted holiday cottages on Tresco, although I'd never dream of telling you which ones. "Why is it," The Editor had asked, "that ghosts usually come from the last few hundred years? We never seem to be visited by our earliest ancestors."

This intrigued us, and I think that it was during the first quarter of the bottle that we decided that Early, or Neolithic, Man touches us in a subtler way, through the works he has left on the landscape. A message written large. On Scilly you will see the remains of our ancestors' works from over 4,000 years ago – the most concentrated grouping in Europe. Some are utilitarian, like field systems – but most are ritualistic, like graves, mounds, spine walls and standing stones.

These constructions have lasted in a kind of sacred landscape which is most evident on the North End of Tresco, and on Shipman's Head on Bryher. Although Mesolithic Man left his mark on West Cornwall from around 4,000 BC, Scilly's chambered cairns and entrance graves are Neolithic – dating from about 2,500 BC onwards.

SYMPATHETIC AND SPIRITUAL MAGIC
"Can you imagine," mused the Editor "the effort that they expended in shifting those huge slabs of granite onto the top of each cairn? And some of them never even contained a burial."

These chambered cairns were similar, we decided, to churches – communally built stone structures where the burial of the dead was a subsidiary event.

Like churches they were focal points to signal the affiliation, piety and wealth of the groups who built them – and the core of a sympathetic and spiritual magic linked to the land and its fertility.

The North End, where many of these constructions are located is wild and uncultivated. The field walls define burial grounds, and possibly link family sepulchres in a network of relationships... on the landscape as in life. The Editor claims to be able to start at Piper's Hole and trace a line marked by stones that leads through several tumuli, The (Victorian) Monument, Oliver's Battery and on to Star Castle on St Mary's. Here was an Early British society that believed strongly in life-after-death and the immortality of the soul.

Archaeologists have never found evidence of any social hierarchy on Scilly before the 17th century. For centuries, Scilly may have been a place of burial, a ritualistic landscape occupied by priests, priestesses and the spirits of ancestors who – it was believed – were unable to cross water to haunt their descendants on the mainland.

Scilly was a single land-mass (except St Agnes) until Norman times when the sea started its invasion, and it wasn't until Tudor times that all the various islands were created. The Romans used a harbour in between what is now St Martin's and the Eastern Isles. A significant Romano-British shrine or beacon was found nearby on Nour Nour – probably dedicated to Vesta.

It was during the last half of the Malt bottle that the Editor spoke of one of the oldest of British legends – the visit of the teenage Jesus to Cornwall and Somerset with his Mother and great-uncle Joseph of Arimathea. "Documents in many great libraries speak of it," said the Editor, "which doesn't mean it's true. But who says there is never any truth in folklore?"

Here's just part of the old story he told me as we sat by the fire – a tale that inspired William Blake to write *Jerusalem*:

After invading Britain, the Romans discovered the tin mines in Cornwall, and lead and pewter in the Mendips. Until then they had dealt through middle-men – Jews or Phoenicians. The many Jewish place-names in Cornwall and the West Country hint at an ancient connection. British chieftains, or Kings, controlled the mines, and St Anne – mother of the Virgin Mary – is said to have been a Princess of Cornish or Breton royal blood. Joseph of Arimathea, Mary's uncle, was described as a "noble decurion" – a rank sometimes applied to a powerful official in charge of mines and metal-trading.

ST JOSEPH, THE GRAIL, KING ARTHUR

The Druid religion with its emphasis on the soul's immortality may have had a profound effect on the family. Grail legends focus on Glastonbury and Cornwall – sites for metal trading and both centres of much older Druid traditions. Was Jesus introduced to the Old Ways – Druidism – by his great-uncle and relatives of his Celtic grandmother?

After the Crucifixion, Joseph of Arimathea is said to have been sent by St Philip from Gaul to Britain with the Cup from the Last Supper – the Holy Grail. It is said that he was welcomed with 12 of his followers by King Arviragus – ancestor of Lear and Coel – and was granted land at Glastonbury where he built the first church and converted the Britons to Christianity.

The Druids apparently accepted this new Celtic Christianity seamlessly, 450 years before St Augustine came to convert a later invader – the pagan Saxon. Later the Celtic Church was overwhelmed by the Roman Church's stern doctrine of unquestioning faith and obedience to an infallible Pope. But an older, gentler quest for truth through knowledge of oneself – gnosis – still echoes through the Grail Legends.

The Celtic Church clung to life in the far west of England, in Ireland, in Wales, on Scottish islands, and here in Scilly. King Arthur, and every one of the Knights of the Round Table, were said to be blood descendants of Joseph of Arimathea and therefore related to Jesus. They were inspired to seek the Grail and thus self-knowledge. It was only attainable by the pure in heart.

"Wouldn't it be wonderful," my friend concluded, "if on the way to Cornwall the Bethany Family had stopped at Scilly? Perhaps they did. Perhaps a teenage Jesus stood on these cliffs, just as we have done, and perhaps he wondered at the beauty of the place and the number of graves that even then were thousands of years old.

Maybe King Arthur – a reputed descendant of Joseph, as were all the Knights of the Round Table – was buried here later... Who knows what secrets lie underfoot? Sweet food for the imagination.

There's so much more to tell – but it's late, and the Malt has run out..."

Insular Things 3

I'M TERSE SCOT – MICE OR TESTS?

From the earliest moment of human enlightenment, schools of philosophy have sought illumination of hidden truths. Pythagoreans, Platonists, Druids, mediaeval transcendental magicians, Cabalists, Masons and Gnostics all strove for a method whereby incommunicable knowledge might be revealed to the inner mind.

The art of Geometry revealed proportion and numerical relationships. The Egyptian (and later Greek) art of Gematria extended the range of literary language by attributing a numerical value to each letter of the alphabet. Thus the numbers of sacred names and words could be combined in a literary algebra to reveal greater insight into the Meaning of Life.

SO STIR ME, ETC...

One of the great things about living on Tresco is that one has the time to wander lonely along the beach, kicking stones and thinking great thoughts... like 'why are we here?' and 'what are anagrams for?' What inner truths might be demonstrated by re-arranging the letters of some well-known names and phrases? If you turn to the greatest encyclopedia in the world – the Internet – you'll discover that hundreds of people with time on their hands were there before you. Their works illuminate dark corners of hidden knowledge and are extremely clever – one or two achieve a harmonious perfection which places them on the highest plane of philosophical enlightenment.

CORSET MITES

Here are some simple and mildly amusing examples to start with. 'The Morse Code' enigmatically re-forms itself as 'Here Comes Dots', while 'A Decimal Point' is 'I'm A Dot In Place'. More controversially, 'Evangelist' becomes 'Evil's Agent'. Moving right along, 'Desperation' sinisterly changes to 'A Rope Ends It'. Some anagrams contain a dreadful warning – 'Slot Machines' becomes

'Cash Lost In 'em', others display blinding glimpses of the obvious – 'Semolina' becomes 'Is No Meal'.

Well-known people have some appropriate, even prophetic, anagrams: 'Tony Blair' famously switches both to 'Tory in Lab' and 'Not by Rail', while 'Alec Guinness' could only be 'Genuine Class'. Our own dear Curator 'Mike Nelhams' becomes 'I'm shaken Elm'. Shockingly, 'President Clinton of the USA' dissolves into 'To copulate he finds Interns'. 'My known CIA lies' comes from 'Monica Lewinsky'. And how extraordinary that 'Mother in Law' should become 'Woman Hitler'.

And what about the mystical harmony of 'Eleven plus Two' changing to 'Twelve plus One'? Transcendental, man...

ESCORT'S ITEM

Let us move into the world of Super-Anagrams. Some of these are amazing and have surely been devised by the sort of person who is brilliant at Scrabble, and who can complete the *Tresco Times* cross-word over breakfast.

We all remember one of the most famous, albeit contrived, quotations of the 20th century – 'That's one small step for a man, one giant leap for mankind.' Neil Armstrong. Someone has re-worked it to provide the following Super-Anagram: 'Man left planet, makes a large stride, ran, pins thin flag on Moon. On to Mars!'.

...'TIS MERE COST

But for a truly amazing finale, how about this? Possibly the best known piece of English ever written..... 'To be or not to be: that is the question, whether 'tis nobler in the mind to suffer the slings and arrows of outrageous fortune.' This yields the following insight, a Super Anagram of world-class quality – 'In one of the Bard's best-thought-of tragedies, our insistent hero, Hamlet, queries on two fronts about how life turns rotten.' Says it all, really.

Should it occur to you that the headings in this piece all seem to be non sequitors – well, try the anagram. Come, it rests... *Tresco Times*.

TIMBER GALORE!

Amidst scenes reminiscent of that famous film *Whisky Galore!* islanders were busy in January hauling vast numbers of the finest pitch pine planks from the beaches.

Astonishingly, no one quite knows where it came from. A ship somewhere between the Bristol Channel and Biscay must have jettisoned its load of prime timber, and the sea delivered it to Scilly – and later to the coast of Cornwall.

Tresco Estate owns the flotsam and jetsam washed onto its beaches and this unexpected bounty was immediately put to good use in the New Inn. Visitors will now find a magnificent new bar constructed with extravagant use of wood. All over Scilly, book-shelves and cottage extensions sprouted, as boats vied to steer the harvest home to the appropriate island.

January is a month when local fishermen stay at home rather than face the rough seas which batter the islands at this time of year. This January every man with a boat in the water hauled in a profitable catch of wood and many post-Christmas bills were paid early. The good news didn't end there. To celebrate the opening of the bar, Mr Dorrien Smith provided free beer on the first night to celebrate our unexpected good fortune – and the creation of a really splendid drinking and eating place.

We then all drank to the anonymous skipper who had provided the wood, and to Fate that had delivered it to Tresco.

TRESCO TIMES WINNING CIRCULATION WAR

Our circulation has now risen to 25,000 – about a quarter of that of Mr Murdoch's *Times* – and it costs our readers nothing. A rattled Mr Murdoch has now reduced his *Times* to just 25p a copy. Will it soon be free? Will he post it to you like we do? Where will it all end?

RICHARD'S BIG DAY OUT

Richard Chuter, who drives the tractor that pulls the cottage "bus", recently had an interesting trip to St Mary's on his day off. He went over in his punt

– a dinghy with an outboard – and tied up on the Quay. After lunch he decided to return home, but had trouble starting the outboard.

The St Mary's Harbourmaster asked him to move to let a tripper boat in, so Richard drifted off and dropped anchor in the harbour. Eventually the engine started and Richard began his voyage back to Tresco. All the way back the engine played up – smoking and overheating to the extent that Richard was barely making way. Instead of 20 minutes, it took him hours to reach Cam Near. It was there that he noticed the great raft of seaweed keeping station directly astern of him. Then he realised... he had forgotten to haul up the anchor.

CULTURE CLASH!

Some of our visitors can seem to be a bit peculiar at times – but it never occurred to us that our ways might appear rather strange to mainland folk. This is about Chris Potterton – the shaggy-maned artist from Bryher. Chris has become long-sighted over the years, and made an appointment with an optician in Penzance. The optician fitted him up with some spectacles and Chris stepped out of the shop into the sunshine.

For the first time in many years everything appeared sharp and in focus, all the colours bright and clear. He admits that he became a bit ecstatic – wandering down the street gazing at the clouds, the trees and the buildings – and murmuring softly "It's all so beautiful!" and "I can see, I can see!" This soon attracted the attention of a large policeman who promptly felt Chris's collar.

The copper was convinced that he had nicked someone high on something other than the joys of life. Having established that his suspect was called Chris Potterton he asked him to empty his pockets. First out was a lock-knife, familiar to all of us who own a boat. "Offensive weapon" said the policeman. Next was a store-card and a signed blank cheque in the name of Chris Hopkins – proprietor of Fraggle Rock on Bryher. "Thought you said your name was Potterton" growled the copper "we'd better discuss this at the police station".

The neighhourly thing on the off-islands is to lend cards to friends who don't have them – or to friends who may shop for you while in Penzance. The mainland seems to lag behind in the concept of communal cards – the large policeman certainly had trouble getting his head round it.

Chris tried to be helpful "Why not call Chris Hopkins at Fraggle Rock?" As the policeman dialled the number, a tiny cloud crossed the sunny landscape of Chris's mind... and started to grow. Something – he couldn't quite remember what – plucked at the memory. He heard the voice answer the phone, and then he remembered.

Chris Hopkins had left a new receptionist from the mainland in charge. "Do you know a Chris Potterton?" asked the policeman. "I am afraid not...." came the reply. Thunder, lightning and torrential rain now swept Chris's mental vistas, where once had been sunshine.

He was finally released several hours later – thanks to the intervention of the optician who vouched for his patient... and for his unconventional insular ways.

CHAPTER TWENTY SIX

THE *TRESCO GUARDIAN*

In 1997, I underook an editorial exchange with Shift Control – the on-line magazine of the *Guardian*. I enjoyed my week in London, and a great deal of what I learned was later applied to Tresco's own website. (In fact only the *Guardian* and the *Telegraph* beat the *Tresco Times* to an electronic on-line edition. Mr Murdoch followed later. For a glorious six months Yahoo! listed the *Tresco Times* as an on-line national newspaper next to the *Telegraph*).

Rada Petrovic – editor of the on-line *Guardian* – spent a week on Tresco, and we printed a supplement to the *Tresco Times* – the *Tresco Guardian* which she edited. Here are some extracts:

THE TRESCO GUARDIAN
The On-line Guardian Editor comes to Tresco

By Rada Petrovic

At the end of May 1997, Richard Barber, editor of the Tresco Times, *came to the* Guardian's *New Media Lab in London as part one of a friendly journalistic "exchange". The swap was triggered by a Sunday morning spent perusing the papers, when a certain article on Tresco set my curiosity racing. The following Monday, a Net Search revealed that Tresco had a website, a print publication, and an editor to boot. It wasn't long before I picked up the phone and a deal was struck. The aim of the exchange was a simple one: to share knowledge and stimulate some new material for our respective publications.*

During his secondment in our department – the Internet arm of the national newspaper – Richard had a bird's-eye view of how we build the Guardian *website and threw a few wise words into the weekly online magazine*

Shift Control – which I have the dubious pleasure of editing. I would hope that what Richard learned will eventually be of use in expanding and refining the online version of the Tresco Times.

My stay, two months later, took a slightly different form: an exploration, geographical and cultural, of a highly individualistic island. The results of that exploration and the words it inspired follow. I hope it makes for interesting reading. I certainly had a most stimulating stay on Tresco.

What does a first-time visitor find most appealing?
Rada chooses her favourite moments...

MY TOP 10 ISLAND TREASURES
Everyone who lives on – or has visited Tresco has their favourite hangouts. After careful deliberation, I designated the following as my top 10 island experiences:

1. Pentle Bay
I brought a friend to Pentle Bay who is familiar with the some of the finer stretches of Caribbean coastline. I thought she would be an accurate barometer of

Pentle Bay.

how idyllic this bay really is. She began to gush like a tourist brochure. Best late in the day when the tide is coming in and that other person has gone home.

2. The night sky

As I write this in Gadwall, I am awaiting the pitch black night to fall so that I can watch the stars. In the city, stars are at a premium: our expectations are so low that we hardly ever raise our heads to see what's going on in the skies above. I saw the Pole Star for the first time here, and the Milky Way. Cosmic, dare I say, on a clear night.

3. Abbey Drive at speed

Possibly because it's the road to (you guessed it) Pentle Bay, or possibly because it's just an elegant, shady, meandering lane, Abbey Drive is best enjoyed while you are cycling full speed and the wind is whistling through your hair. The island tractor-bus is a good alternative, preferably packed with a jolly crowd.

Abbey Drive.

St Nicholas Church graveyard.

4. Tregarthen Hill

A wild and woolly spot, testament to Tresco's schizophrenic landscape. Good for a 'Scott of the Antarctic' moment as you survey the heights you have risen to – and the land at your feet. The springy peat is all the better to stride purposefully and energetically to the summit.

5. St Nicholas Church graveyard

I cannot resist those old lichen-covered tomb-stones where you can hardly read the inscription. In this graveyard, practically every slab of stone has been gnawed away, and you can ramble on the grass without fear of upsetting someone's turmoiled spirit.

6. The silence
I live in an environmental area in London which doesn't even come close to the tranquillity of Tresco. It is a relief not to hear police sirens, the distant hum of the main road, car alarms, the thud-thud-thud of someone's stereo... the cacophony that clatters in the background every day and night.

7. The deck of the Island Hotel
The place for a decadent moment, accessorized with a Bloody Mary. Gazing vacantly into the middle distance you think you could be Audrey Hepburn and it's the Cote d'Azur. Don't be silly, it's only Tresco.

The deck of the Island Hotel.

8. Abbey Gardens
Loathe as I am to cite such an obvious landmark, the Abbey Gardens has to have a mention because it's the closest I'll get to my vision of a magical, secret garden. Standing at the top of Neptune's Steps, one can entertain delusions of grandeur, ie, a midsummer evening's party, string quartet... you get the picture.

Abbey gardens.

9. The New Inn staff
I like places where a bottle of wine misordered finds its way to the kitchen staff. In addition to common sense in the face of adversity, these people score points on professional, but not overbearing, service – and a sense of humour.

10. My cottage Gadwall
The comfort zone after a hard day's pondering.

The New Inn.

NOTES AND QUERIES – a regular **Guardian** feature, is a hotbed of speculative trivia (or profound knowledge) supplied by curious readers. My own island investigations dredged up a number of intellectual curiosities. In the tradition of Notes & Queries, you are most welcome to supply your own version of the truth.

1. The waters around Tresco are crystal clear because:
a) Scilly is a pollution-free zone
b) The islands lie outside the Boreal region
c) The Estate does a rigorous job of cleaning up

2. Which Tresco cave has a candlelit entrance and a large freshwater lake?
a) Piper's Hole
b) Devil's Hole
c) Gun Hole

The cottage at Gadwell.

3. *In January, Scilly enjoys a higher average monthly temperature than:*
a) *London*
b) *Cannes*
c) *Corsica*

4. *Historical rumour has it that 18th century Scillonians encouraged ship-wrecks by:*
a) *Tying lights to the tails of cows along the coast*
b) *Sending the lighthouse-keeper home early*
c) *This is a heinous lie: Scillonians only save, never wreck, lives*

5. *In the winter months, the island's primary source of income is:*
a) *The* Tresco Times
b) *Narcissi*
c) *Fishing*

6. *In 1651, Cromwell's Castle was built. What was its purpose?*
a) *To house exiles from the mainland*
b) *To defend the channel between New Grimsby and Bryher*
c) *To store Scilly's supply of gunpowder*

7. *When did the Celtic dialect of Cornwall die out in Scilly?*
a) *The 18th century*
b) *The 17th century*
c) *The Middle Ages*

8. *Where on Tresco lie the ruins of St Nicholas Abbey?*
a) *Beneath St Nicholas Church*
b) *In the Abbey Gardens*
c) *In the Abbey itself*

9. *The Scillies first helicopter service began operating in?*
a) *1954*
b) *1964*
c) *1974*

10. *Tresco's cut flowers were first dispatched to Covent Garden in:*
a) *Air-conditioned cargo*
b) *A lined, wooden box which was packed with ice*
c) *A hat box*

Answers 1a, 2a, 3b, 4a, 5b, 6b, 7a, 8b, 9b, 10c.

CHAPTER TWENTY SEVEN
FUNERAL

She was elderly – in her late seventies – and she died quite suddenly on a bright spring afternoon. The last thing she must have seen was the sunlit harbour, and the last thing she would have heard was the sound of the birds and the mewing of the seagulls. The scent of cut grass was in her nostrils since they had cut the verges that very afternoon. For her it was not such a bad death.

For her family left behind it was hard, and the community knew that; their concern was for her children and grandchildren and it was demonstrated in small acts of kindness. No one was maudlin or sentimental. They were sad because she had been well-liked, loved even. But on Tresco the veil between life and death is thin.

So life went on much the same for everyone over the rest of the week.

The funeral was at 2 o'clock in the church of St Nicholas that sits at the bottom of the hill in Dolphin Town. It has a quiet and loving atmosphere. Like many places where good people congregate it has absorbed beautiful thoughts and prayers in its very stones and gives them back to anyone sensitive enough to receive them. It is a place deeply cared for, and is well looked after by the community. It has a purpose.

As islanders gathered before the service, chatting in the graveyard, the sun came out. Everyone had changed into their Sunday best, the men in suits and jackets that had not been worn since the last funeral or wedding, running a finger round a shirt collar too tight against the neck. The women, also in black, were much more put-together. Somehow every woman seems to have a dark outfit that fits her.

Everyone takes their place in the church. Suddenly we are awkward, eyes are averted. The time is coming to say goodbye. The coffin, covered in flowers stands before the choir. We sit, each immersed in contemplation of mortality. Robert and Lucy take their places in the family pew. Six men of the island sit next to them in dark suits. They are pall-bearers. They look nervous.

It's a mixed congregation. Honest faces, tanned or weathered – from all the islands. The youngsters blooming in health. Older ones moving slowly. Some latecomers arrive, straight from their jobs and still in work-clothes. The undertaker shows them to the last seats in the congregation. Then he returns, leading the family to their pews in the front. Was there ever such a dignified undertaker? With white hair and beard he looks like God. Nothing escapes him, his care and solicitude for the bereaved, his whole body language – everything about him encapsulates why we are here.

Finally, all are seated and our vicar Donald Marr starts the service. He knows each of us well. He will bind us together, express our feelings, focus our sympathy for the bereaved. He starts by reminding us of the beauty of our surroundings, outside and in. He tells us that we are here to celebrate a life...

It is a simple service, and it is right. We sing the hymns that she loved and which we all know. Emotion starts to be released... How Great Thou Art! Tresco's Headmaster reads the lesson. Then prayers, resonating with the poetry of ritual, full of comfort. Then we are singing again. Bread of Heaven! Donald speaks from the pulpit. His words are well chosen. We all knew her well; there is no need to express anything but the simple love and affection that we all hold. It is well done.

A long moment of silent contemplation, more prayers and then the final hymn. Donald advances to the coffin, blesses her. There is a deep, deep tension. This is goodbye.

The undertaker returns. A nod of his head, and the pall-bearers take up their places. Their wooden carrying bars slide into the strops. They take the strain, the undertaker removes the trestles under the coffin, and slowly – ever so slowly and carefully – the pall-bearers turn until they face the congregation. The organ plays The Old Rugged Cross as Donald and the undertaker lead the way. Behind them, with down-cast eyes, the pall-bearers walk the coffin still covered in flowers, through the congregation to the door at the back of the church. The island is saying goodbye and many are in tears.

The family leave the church, and we follow. Outside, she is lowered gently into the warm earth of Tresco to lie next to others who went before her. Handfuls of earth are tossed into the grave. Donald speaks the final words of comfort and commitment. We watch from a distance as the family say their last farewells.

Standing outside the church in the sunshine, friends from other islands – not seen for a while – greet each other. Conversation starts. Quiet, still reverent.

Soon we walk to the Hotel behind the family. Under a canopy, drinks and sandwiches are served. The family circulate, talking to friends, shaking hands, hugging. There's relief in the air. The island has said goodbye. Laughter is heard again.

For those that are left, life must go on – and that is just as it should be.

CHAPTER TWENTY EIGHT

THE LAW OF THE ISLAND

Obey the Law of the Island, it's old and as clear as the sea
Passed on by those before us – a lesson for you and for me

Two thirds of Scilly is water, two thirds of the world the same.
A third we tend and look after, the rest can never be tame

Look up at the Moon and thank her as through the clouds she rides
Hers are the rhythms we follow in step with the sea and the tides.

The very First Law of the Island Is 'Honour thy Mother the Sea'
For Life came first from the ocean – bloodline of you and of me.

Make peace with the Lord of the Ocean, for Neptune rules our domain
And when he meets the Sou' Wester we bow to the storm and the rain.

We live by the sea, and on the sea, and some of us fish the Deep
It's a happy life and a healthy life and one that we wish to keep.

But forget not that Man's a spoiler, it's been thus ever since Cain,
So don't fish all of the shoal, boys, leave some to come back again.

Our islands share no borders save with the sea and the skies,
And when the sea invades us it's always the land that dies.

Remember when you fill up with petrol or the fire roars up the flue:
That Nature demands repayment and sometimes from other than you.

The fuel that you burn on the mainland warms up our climate as well
Then there's more of the sea and less of the land and Paradise turns to Hell.

This is the beginning-and-end of the Law, the warp and the weft of the weave:
Think what you do, how it is done and what sort of mess you may leave.

Of an Island Race is each Briton and we used to heed these things
Before motorways and suburbia and all that Modern Life brings......

Obey the Law of the Island, my Child, it's old and as clear as the sea,
Leave it for those who come after – a message from you and from me.

THE COMMODORE

Postscript

This book has been a personal look at some events past and present that appealed to me. It is a perspective from one pair of eyes. Others may see things differently. It is a mere handful of sand from a whole strand of stories and events – much more has been left out than has been included.

The *Tresco Times* itself is an on-going magazine that tells its readers about what is happening on the island and recalls the past that forms the present. Often readers write in with corrections and additions to stories that we print. In this way history is written; by people who were there or have a reason to know better than this poor scribe.

I hope that readers who find things wrong in this book will write with corrections, additions or enlargements on events that I have described.

For I am sure that there will be a sequel. There's still so much to tell.

At **www.islandrace.com** you can comment publicly, or email us privately. A Limited Editon reproduction of Graeme Spence's magnificent 1792 'Survey of the Scilly Isles', mentioned in Chapter Three, is also available on-line. If you love Scilly and want to contribute stories, corrections, memories or photographs then please do so.

With best wishes

RICHARD BARBER and 'THE COMMODORE'
Tresco, TR24 0PW

SUBSCRIBERS

Loes M. Abrahams, Bristol
Robert Ackland, Blackheath, London
James Ackland, Bristol
Janet Adams, Sedgley
Eva and Derek Aldred, Rochdale,
    Lancashire
Patrick Ramsay Andrew
Mr Johnny Armstrong, Brancepeth,
    Durham
Mike Ashley, Falmouth, Cornwall
Peter and Denise Aspinall, Flitwick,
    Beds
Roger Bade, Morden, Surrey
Stan and Wendy Badham,
    Dodford Priory, Worcestershire
Mr and Mrs C.H. Baines,
    Penmaenmawr
The Baker Family, Sandy Lane
    (week 14), Tresco
Bat and Ball, Barton, Warwickshire
Alan and Madeleine Baptist, Truro,
    Cornwall
Robin Barbour, Dorset
Robert, Rowena, Lydia and Maisie
    Barlow, Cambridge
David Barnard, Isle of Wight
Michael R. Barnes, Bath
Mr and Mrs John Bates,
    Crowthorne, Berkshire
Sylvia I. Bates, Culmstock, Devon
Kim Beazley (née Clements),
    Tregony, Cornwall
Roger and Molly Bird, Finchley,
    London
Geoffrey John Birks, Broom,
    Warwickshire
Mr D. I. Birley, Oadby,
    Leicestershire
Margaret Bowden, Finchley,
    London
Nicholas Bowlby
Ann and Duncan Boxall, Malvern,
    Worcestershire
Julie Brett, Mersea Island, Essex
Stephen and Janet Briggs,
    Much Marcle, Herefordshire
Patricia M. Brindley, Swanage,
    Dorset
Anne Buchanan (née Chudleigh),
    Penzance, Cornwall

Chester C. Burley III, Fairfield,
    Connecticut, USA
Andrew J. Burt, Inkberrow,
    Worcestershire
Brian Burton, Newbury, Berkshire
Kay Cartwright, Wilmslow,
    Cheshire
Theresa Carver (née Clements),
    St Ives, Cornwall
Wingate Charlton
Eddie Charlton
Sarah and Marshall Christie,
Dr Joan Clarke, Highcliffe, Dorset
Anthony V. Claydon, East Knoyle,
    Wiltshire
Mr Kerry Clements, Fraddon,
    Cornwall
Mrs Ivy Clements, St Ives, Cornwall
John and Sue Cluley, Laverton,
    Nr Broadway, Worcestershire
Mrs Joyce Clutterbuck (née
    Handy), Dial Rocks, Tresco
The Cocking Family, Yarnton,
    Oxon
Jean Cook, Forfar, Scotland
Marjorie H. Coombe, Penzance,
    Cornwall
Lynn and Ann Cooper,
    Crowthorne, Berkshire
Mr and Mrs James Dorrien Smith,
    London
John E. Coote, Dorridge, Solihull
Anna and Charles Cowley,
Barbara and Brian Critchley,
    Widnes, Cheshire
Mandy de Haan, Salcombe, Devon
The Dean Family, Alderley Edge,
    Cheshire
Gerry Dobbs, Yorkshire
Iris Donoghue, Lindfield,
    West Sussex
David Dowrick, Hayle, Cornwall
Mrs Joan Doyle, Marazion, Cornwall
Gerald and Sheila Drew
Helen Edgeley, Firsdown, Salisbury,
    Wiltshire
Naomi and Chris Edwards,
    Wedmore, Somerset
Julian R. B. Edwards, Camberley,
    Surrey

David J. Eldered, Chatham, Kent
George and Rosie Ellison, Little
    Flushing, Cornwall
Rachel Eyre, Ogston, Derbyshire
Neil and Lesley Farmer, Long
    Buckby, Northampton
Robert Q. Fay, Stockland, Devon
Elizabeth Fenley, London
Anne and Tony Ferguson
Clive and Kathy Fidgeon, Foscot,
    Oxfordshire
Southern Finance, Southampton
Bob Finch, Kimpton,
    Hertfordshire
Michael and Jenny Foot, Iford, East
    Sussex
Nicholas Fridd, Wells, Somerset
Ivy H. Galloway, Kenilworth,
    Warwickshire
Geoff Giddy, Bideford, Devon
Gill Pope and Mike Glover,
    Bideford, Devon
David Good, Tewkesbury
Stuart E. Goode, Shepleigh Court,
    Devon
Colin E. Goodenough, Reading,
    Berkshire
Alan and Ann Goymer, Wookey
    Hole, Somerset
Rita G. Green, Chideock, Dorset
Ken and Shirley Green,
    Whissendine, Rutland
Mr and Mrs M. Green-Armytage,
    Sheffield
Mr and Mrs J. Green-Armytage,
    Warwickshire
Alison Greene, Holcombe Rogus,
    Somerset
C. M. Grigg, Harpenden,
    Hertfordshire
M. Groves, St Mary's, Isles of Scilly
Mr and Mrs A. H. Haley, St Clears,
    Carmarthen
N. Haley, St Martins
Richard and Marion Halfpenny,
    Horsham, West Sussex
Gordon and Judith Hall, Alderley
    Edge, Cheshire
Marian and Roger Hancock,
    Banbury, Oxon

Mr and Mrs Ralph Handy, St Mary's, Isles of Scilly

Mike Harcum, Kingsbury, London NW9

Brian and Barbara Hardiman, Exmouth, Devon

Mrs Patricia Harding

Lt Col. And Mrs I. V. K. Harris,

Brian Hartley, Bury, Lancashire

Jim Hawkings, Credenhill, Herefordshire

Mr and Mrs R.J. Herd, Warwickshire

Bruce Hewett, Budleigh Salterton, Devon

Mr Richmond Heywood, Penzance, Cornwall

Nigel H. M. Hogg, Blaisdon, Gloucestershire

Charlotte Holman, London and Seaspray

Edward Holman, London and Seaspray

Henry Holman, London and Seaspray

James and Fiona Holman, London and Seaspray

Mrs Megan Holt-Thomas, Chelwood Gate, East Sussex

Jean Hopkins, Gressenhall, Norfolk

Betty Horrell, Longthorpe, Peterborough

David and Frances Howard-Pearce, Weir Quay, Devon

Roy Hudd

Susie Hug, Winchester, Hampshire

Mrs Glenys R. Hurle-Hobbs, Chichester, West Sussex

Mr B. Hyner, Birmingham

John and Olwyn Iles, Swansea

Duncan and Nikki Irvin, Brussels, Belgium

Kate and Husky Irvin, Somerset and The Scillies

Tina and Ian Irvin, Taunton, Somerset

P. N. Jackson, Acton, W3

Dr and Mrs Peter Jameson, Connecticut, U.S.A.

James P. Jenkin DIP. HORT. KEW., Blackpool, Dartmouth, Devon

Dennis Trevellick Jenkins, Liskeard, Cornwall

John Jobson, Cornish Avenue, Tresco/Victoria, Australia

Mrs Linda and Ms Amy Juhala, Bismarck, North Dakota, USA

Sam and Tom Karkeek, St Mawgan, Cornwall

Stewart, Bee and Zoë Lang, Bristol

Ted and Amy Langdon, Bryher

Wing Cmdr G.R. Leatherbarrow, St Marys

Leslie A. Leney, Royal Observer Corps. 19 Group V4 Ruxley Tower, Claygate

Revd Jay and Revd Mary Pat Lennard, Falkirk

Mr and Mrs D. Levitt, Luton, Bedfordshire

Anthony V. S. Lewington, Martley, Worcestershire

Roy Lewis, Brixham, Devon

Anne Lewis-Smith

Sidney and Betty Lindsell, Sidcup, Kent

Joan Llewelyn, Dorset

Jeremy Llewelyn, Surrey

Elizabeth Lloyd, Ramsbury, Wiltshire

Famille Lomenech, Paris, France

Eileen and Jack Lonergan, Charlesworth, Derbyshire

Betty Lusty, Hove, Sussex

Pearl Lyon, Barton-on-Sea, Hampshire

Sheila and Henry Macintosh, Camberley, Surrey

Patrick and Elona Macintosh, Sherborne, Dorset

Mr and Mrs I. W. Mackay, South Tehidy, Camborne, Cornwall

Mrs Glenys Mackie (née Venn), a Scillonhan, Wales

John and Ann Manley, Weston-super-Mare, Somerset

Stephanie M. Marsh, Bispham Green, Lancashire

Helen Marshall, Lindfield, West Sussex

Katherine A. Martinez, Henley-on-Thames, Oxon

Brenda Maskell (née Franklin), Brighton, Sussex

Sheila and Barry Matthews, Evesham, Worcestershire

Nigel J. Mattison, Bishop's Stortford, Hertfordshire

Paul and Denise Mayne, Bedford, NY, U.S.A.

David McCarthy, Kinross, Scotland

Dr Paul McCloskey, Little Hadham, Hertfordshire

Dorothy McIsaac, Falmouth, Cornwall/Houston, TX, USA

William and Lillian Mary McLucas, St Mary's, Isles of Scilly

Charles Moore, Nottingham

Thea and David Morris

Thomas A. Morris

Barbara J. Moss, Culmstock, Devon

John and Diane Narbett, Belbroughton, Worcestershire

Rachel E. Need, Henley-on-Thames, Oxon

Keith O. Nicholls, Newton Abbot, Devon

Alan Nicholls, Bristol

Pippa Nickolds, East Clandon, Surrey

Mrs Janis Nightingale, Scilly

Mr and Mrs W. Norris, Lower Daggons, Hampshire

Pat and Liz Nurden, Tewkesbury, Gloucestershire

Didier G. Olivry, La Membrolle, France

Philip H. Owen, Levington, Suffolk

M. E. and Mrs M. L. A. Padbury, Norwich, Norfolk

P. S. Padmore Esq., Dummer, Hampshire

Major General T. B. Palmer C.B. (deceased) and Mrs Palmer, Stoke St Gregory, Taunton

Roger A. Parham, Minsterworth, Gloucestershire

Christina and Martin Pay, Isle of Wight

Michelle Peat, London

Arthur W. and Doris K. Periam, Ashley Green, Buckinghamshire

Howard G. Perrin, Wolverhampton

Thomas Pope, Stratton, Dorchester

Christopher Pope, Wrackleford, Dorchester

John and Jeanne Popplewell, Berkshire

Bob Potts, East Hanningfield, Essex

Arthur F. Powis, Loughton, Essex

Winston and Peggy Pritchard, Ilkley, West Yorkshire

Sandy, Greg, Christopher and Oliver Pritchard, Haslemere, Surrey

Barbara and Roy Rainford

R.T. and M.I. Rawsthorne

Mr and Mrs David Rea, Coldharbour, Surrey

B. N. Reckitt, Cumbria

Clive J. Relf, Gloucestershire

Judith E. Richards, Strawberry Hill, Twickenham, Middlesex

Su Riggs, Tresco 1999-2002

Tim Roberts, Guildford, Surrey

Dr David Robertson, Bromsgrove, Worcestershire

Mrs Adrienne C. Robson, St Marys, Isles of Scilly

Fiona Jean Robson, St Marys, Isles of Scilly

B. M. Roe, Staffordshire

Phil and Rhon Rogers, Blewbury, Oxfordshire

Beryl and Derek Rose, Chipstead, Kent

Charles E. Rowe, Hamels, Hertfordshire

Margaret Rudkin, Bournemouth

Professor and Mrs John Salter, Sevenoaks, Kent

Peter and Myra Shapter, Hartley, Plymouth, Devon

Dr and Mrs C. R. Sheard, Addingham, West Yorkshire

Mrs Eleanor Simpson, Llidiartywaun, Montgomeryshire

Fred and Heather Slatter, Tavistock, Devon

Peter and Valerie Sleight, Ipplepen, Devon

Simon Smee, Chichester, West Sussex

Glen Smith, St Leonards-On-Sea, East Sussex

Alison Smith, Wimborne, Dorset

Lynne and Alan Spicer, Ashford, Middlesex

Dr and Mrs J. Spurrier, Northants

Albert Steel, born Tresco, now Surrey

Alan and Patricia Stephenson, Huddersfield, West Yorkshire

Ken and Brenda Stock, Stanford-le-Hope, Essex

Mr and Mrs D. Stokes, Tunley, Somerset

Mark and Sue Summers, Stoke Gabriel, Devon

David C. Sumners, London

Charles and Charlotte Sundquist, Stoke St Gregory

Eunice Sutherland, Beaminster, Dorset

M. and S. Szukowski, Dorsten, Germany

Judith Tadros, Attalla, Truro, Cornwall

Bob and Frances Tagert, Hemerdon, Devon

Mr and Mrs Taylor, Rudyard, Staffordshire

Janet Thomas, Alfriston, East Sussex

Dorelia H. Thompson, Blandford Forum, Dorset

Kit Thomson, Hornchurch, Essex

Graham Tippen, Marden, Kent

Roy Tomlinson, Penn, Wolverhampton

Mr and Mrs Jon Tommey, Hampton, Middlesex

Mr and Mrs J. E. Tong, Farnborough, Hampshire

William Tracy, Sarisbury Green, Hampshire

Nicholas and Carole Treadaway, Oxon

Mrs M. A. Tucker,

Mr and Mrs R. Vine, Itchen Abbas, Hampshire

Chris and Tilly Vacher, Clifton, Bristol

Richard and Anne Vosser, Aldershot, Hampshire

Susan M.W. Walliker,

Brian and Jane Webster, Belbroughton, Worcestershire

Reg J. Webster,

Matt and Rachel Wellsbury, Featherstone, Wolverhampton

Geoff and Sheila Wellsbury, Penkridge, Stafford

Mark Wheatland, Southampton, Hamsphire

Stanley T. White, Fakenham, Norfolk

Mr George White, Slaugham, Sussex

Chris and Cerys Wiggin, Cheltenham, Gloucestershire

Mark and Trish Wightman, Broad Hinton, Swindon

Patricia Williams

G. Stewart Williams, Parwich, Derbyshire

Mike Williams, Stourbridge, West Midlands

Hilary Wilson, Harpenden, Hertfordshire

Nick Wood, Sandygate, Sheffield

Ray Woodage, Rogate, West Sussex

David Woodroffe, Craven Arms, Shropshire

Robert Woodroffe, Buckingham

Anne and Ross Woolfrey, Upleadon, Gloucestershire

Mr Ivor Worthington, Chesterfield, Derbyshire

The Prince of Wales meets islanders.